Locating Legal Certainty in Patent Licensing

Ashish Bharadwaj · Vishwas H. Devaiah ·
Indranath Gupta

Locating Legal Certainty in Patent Licensing

 Springer

Ashish Bharadwaj
O. P. Jindal Global University
Sonepat, Haryana, India

Vishwas H. Devaiah
O. P. Jindal Global University
Sonepat, Haryana, India

Indranath Gupta
O. P. Jindal Global University
Sonepat, Haryana, India

ISBN 978-981-15-0180-7   ISBN 978-981-15-0181-4   (eBook)
https://doi.org/10.1007/978-981-15-0181-4

This Springer imprint is published by the registered company Springer Nature Singapore Pte Ltd.
The registered company address is: 152 Beach Road, #21-01/04 Gateway East, Singapore 189721, Singapore

Acknowledgements

We are extremely grateful to all those who have taken time out of their busy schedule and ensured timely completion of this project. This has been made possible because of the extraordinary efforts of Shruti Bhushan and valuable support of Isha Gaba, Navreet Kaur Rana, Arunima Saraf, Ritesh, Basu Chandola, Ranjan Kumar Basantia and Bhupender Kumar who spent several hours of their precious time towards this project. It is towards all of them we owe our gratitude. We would also like to thank our family and our colleagues at O.P. Jindal Global University (JGU) for their constant encouragement. We admire the unconditional support of our Vice Chancellor, Prof. C. Raj Kumar. Foundations of JIRICO are rooted in his vision and leadership.

DISCLOSURE Opinions expressed in the chapters are independent of any research grants received from governmental, intergovernmental and private organizations. The authors' opinions are personal and are based on their research findings and do not reflect the opinions of their institutional affiliation.

Introduction

We live in an era wherein several disruptive technological innovations have transformed the way we live. The Fourth Industrial Revolution has not only brought changes in the way we communicate with each other, but also how information is collected and used to transform the way we inhabit the spaces, commute, interact in our places of work and places of recreation. The Internet of things (IoT), smart cities, smart homes, and smart equipments have become all pervasive and are constantly exchanging and transmitting information about us, thus enabling technological equipments to learn about our habits and choices. The possibility of constant transmission of information and background chatter seems to be taking place without the humans consciously noticing the same. How this information is used and to what extent aspects of private life of an individual are collected and utilized is possibly a subject matter of discussion that is out of the scope of this book. However, it is important to note that this technological revolution is being facilitated through the modern-day patent system. The creation and protection of intellectual property has resulted in the rapid growth of economies. Technological progress is facilitated through rapid diffusion and adoption of innovations.[1] Intellectual property regimes have always been questioned by opponents as some argue that it also facilitates monopolistic behavior on the part of IP owners. However, the fourth industrial revolution is fueled by the need to have more interoperable devices that can relay and exchange valuable information between devices that might have been protected through patents. It is this interoperability that has forced patent owners to come forward more readily to develop standards by pledging their underlying technologies.

With the increasing need for seamless interconnectivity between products and the requirement of interoperability, jurisdictions across the globe have developed some sort of regulatory mechanisms to govern the licensing agreements for Standard Essential Patent (SEP) licensing. These regulatory mechanisms and policies are

---

[1] Ashish Bharadwaj & Punkhuri Chawla, 'International evidence suggests we understand, embrace and protect intellectual property rights' *Financial Express* (02 August 2017) <https://www.financialexpress.com/opinion/international-evidence-suggests-we-understand-embrace-and-protect-intellectual-property-rights/790381/> accessed 02 December 2020.

undergoing constant changes in the domain of patent licensing. Generally speaking, standards are adopted to reduce transaction costs for implementers and increase interoperability among devices and platforms. Standards make our lives as consumers easier. For instance, a Wi-Fi-enabled smartphone device will connect to a Wi-Fi connection regardless of the jurisdiction. It has happened because Wi-Fi is a standard, which has been unanimously adopted by all stakeholders. There are technical standards adopted through several standard setting organizations, and there are standards adopted through market demands, which have evolved with time. Standard setting organisations (SSOs) play a crucial role in operationalizing a standard. The stages through which a standard is operationalized are often fraught with uncertainty, and a lot depends on the internal structure of an SSO. The most significant contributor to the entire process is the IPR policies adopted by each of these SSOs.

The SSO IPR policies generally require two specific commitments from members who intend to submit their underlying technology toward standard development process. The undertaking provided by a prospective implementer to an SSO is that it will make full disclosures of the existing patents and any pending patent applications that are relevant toward the standards development process. SSO members pledging patents toward standard development process are also under an obligation to issue licenses to all implementers on fair, reasonable, and non-discriminatory (FRAND) terms.[2] This obligation upon the patent holder to issue licenses on FRAND terms would enable implementers to adopt technological standard more readily knowing that they would be able to enter a licensing agreement on fair and reasonable terms. Faster adoption and diffusion of the standard would enable the patent holder to earn royalties from multiple implementers, and this scenario appears to be a win-win situation for all the parties. However, this has turned out to be much more difficult and resulted in complex negotiation of licenses between the parties that has also resulted in expensive legal battles fought in multiple jurisdictions. This book aims to unpack the various elements involved in, policy development process in important jurisdictions, standard development process, and the jurisprudence related to SEP.

Chapter 1 will focus on the legal and policy developments in five jurisdictions—the USA, European Union, China, Japan, and India. The policy development in each of these jurisdictions varies from each other, and a comparative study of these five jurisdictions allows us to have a complete understanding of the patent licensing practices across the globe. Chapter 2 will provide a glimpse of the IPR policies in SSOs in three different jurisdictions, i.e., Europe, the USA, and India. These policies show their diverse nature and often lead to complex end-results. Chapter 3 will examine the scope and wider ramifications of the obligations undertaken by the innovators who participate in the standard development process. It will discuss the jurisprudence developed by the courts on various aspects related to the negotiation of a SEP license agreement and how the FRAND terms are to be interpreted.

---

[2] Gil Ohana & Brad Biddle, The Disclosure of Patents and Licensing Terms in Standards Development *in* Jorge.L. Contreras (eds), *The Cambridge Handbook of Technical Standardization Law: Competition, Antitrust, and Patents* (Cambridge University Press, 2019).

Contents

About the Authors

Dr. Ashish Bharadwaj is a Professor and Dean of the Jindal School of Banking & Finance, and co-director of the Jindal Initiative on Research in IP and Competition (JIRICO) at O.P. Jindal Global University. He previously worked at the Jindal Global Law School in Sonipat, India; Institute for Innovation Research in Tokyo, Japan; and the Max Planck Institute for Innovation and Competition Law in Munich, Germany. He holds LL.M. in Law and Economics (as European Commission's Erasmus Mundus scholar) from Erasmus University Rotterdam, University of Hamburg and Manchester University; and Ph.D. (as Max Planck Society fellow) from the Max Planck Institute for Innovation and Competition Law and Ludwig Maximilians University of Munich (LMU). He has also been awarded the Thomas Edison Innovation Fellowship from the Centre for Intellectual Property & Innovation Policy at Antonin Scalia School of Law, George Mason University (USA). Dr. Bharadwaj writes on technology innovation, intellectual property rights, patent licencing, and the interface of law, economics and new technology.

Dr. Vishwas H. Devaiah is a Professor at the Jindal Global Law School, Executive Director of the Centre for Intellectual Property and Technology Law, and co-director of JIRICO. He holds a Ph.D. from the University of Liverpool, LL.M. from Warwick University, and BAL, LL.B. from Bangalore University. He was the recipient of the IMLAB scholarship, and was awarded the 2015 Microsoft IP Teaching Fellowship to engage with researchers at the University of Washington Law School. His primary areas of interest are copyright law, patent law, health law and biotechnology law. He serves as a reviewer for the *Asian Comparative Law Journal, NUJS Law Review* and the *Indian Journal of Medical Ethics*. He was also the Managing Editor of *JGLS's Flagship Journal, Jindal Global Law Review*, which is published by Springer. He is co-founder of the Initiative for Medicines Access and Knowledge (IMAK), New York.

Dr. Indranath Gupta is a Professor at the Jindal Global Law School and Dean of Research, OPJGU. He is a co-director of JIRICO and a Senior Fellow at the Jindal Institute of Behavioural Sciences. He is currently the Jean-Monnet Chair-Academic

Coordinator for the project 'Multi-dimensional Approaches to the Understanding of the E.U. Data Protection Framework. He holds LL.B. degree from the University of Calcutta, and two LL.M. degrees (taught and research) from the University of Aberdeen, UK, and the University of East Anglia, UK. He obtained his Ph.D. from Brunel University, London. He was appointed as the research collaborator by the Università Bocconi, Milan for a project funded by the European Commission under the 7th Framework Programme. He has published widely in international and national law journals and has authored a number of books. His research areas include copyright, database right, data protection, IT law and the interface of IP and competition law.

Chapter 1
Comparative Analysis of Policy Developments

1 Introduction

Intellectual property protection has enabled several economies to develop their high-tech industries rapidly and usher in new technologies. These developments have enabled countries to create valuable technology-intensive exports in the globalized and interconnected world.[1] Innovation and technological progress have played a vital role in the economic development of such countries. To this end, domestic policy framework, legal context, and the regulatory architecture governing high-tech standard development process, patenting, and commercialisation of high-tech innovation has played an incredibly important role.

With the increasing need for seamless interconnectivity between products and necessity of interoperability, jurisdictions across the globe have developed regulatory mechanisms to govern the licensing agreements for licensing of SEPs. These regulatory mechanisms and policies are undergoing constant change with the frequent challenges that arise in the domain of patent licensing. In this chapter, the focus shall be on the legal and policy developments in five jurisdictions—United States of America, European Union, China, Japan, and India. The policy development in each of these jurisdictions varies from each other, and a comparative study of these five jurisdictions allows us to have a complete understanding of global patent licensing. The following sections shall discuss the relevant policy changes in each of these jurisdictions.

---

[1] Ashish Bharadwaj & Punkhuri Chawla, 'International Evidence Suggests We Understand, Embrace and Protect Intellectual Property Rights' Financial Express (2 August 2017) <https://www.financialexpress.com/opinion/international-evidence-suggests-we-understand-embrace-and-protect-intellectual-property-rights/790381/> accessed 02 December 2020.

© The Author(s) 2023
V. H. Bharadwaj et al., *Locating Legal Certainty in Patent Licensing*,
https://doi.org/10.1007/978-981-15-0181-4_1

2 India

2.1 Overview of the Indian Patent System

The Indian Patent system is currently governed by the Patents Act, 1970 which succeeds the Indian Patents and Designs Act, 1911. The 1970 Act brought about multiple amendments as per the recommendations of the Justice N. Rajagopala Ayyangar Committee. The Patents Act, 1970 disallowed product patents on medicines and chemical fertilizers, reduced the process patents on chemicals, and empowered the Patent Controller to grant compulsory license.[2]

As a part of the larger WTO commitments, India agreed to comply with the TRIPS Agreement, which came into force from January 1, 1995. India amended its patent laws to comply with the TRIPS Agreement in 1999, 2002, and again in 2005. Through these amendments incremental changes were made to the Patents Act to comply with the TRIPS mandate.[3]

The Central Government is empowered under the Patents Act to make relevant rules to implement the Act.[4] Patent Rules were amended in 2003 and 2016 in order to keep up with the changes to the Patents Act.[5]

2.2 Indian Law and Licensing

For a discussion on Standard Essential Patents and licensing, it is essential to analyze Chapter XVI of the Patent Act, 1970 with a special focus on Section 84, and Chapter XXIII with a special focus on Section 140. Chapter XVI contains the following sections:

- Section 84 deals with compulsory license. Any person may apply for the grant of a compulsory license of a patent provided the patent is not reasonably accessible in India, or not worked in in India, or not available at a reasonable price.
- Section 85 provides for revocation of patents by the Controller for non-working of the patents in India. If the patented product is not reasonably available in India

---

[2] Uday S Racherla, 'Historical Evolution of India's Patent Regime and Its Impact on Innovation in the Indian Pharmaceutical Industry' in KC Liu & Uday S Racherla (eds), *Innovation, Economic Development, and Intellectual Property in India and China* (Springer 2019).

[3] V Manickavasagam, *Intellectual Property Rights and The Impact of Trips Agreement with Reference to Indian Patent Law* (Planning Commission, O15012/3/02-SER 2007) <https://niti.gov.in/plannningcommission.gov.in/docs/reports/sereport/ser/ser_alla.pdf> accessed 02 December 2020.

[4] Office of the Controller General of Patents, *Designs and Trademark History of Indian Patent System* <http://www.ipindia.nic.in/history-of-indian-patent-system.htm> accessed 02 December 2020.

[5] Office of the Controller General of Patents, *Frequently Asked Questions 2020* http://www.ipindia.nic.in/writereaddata/Portal/Images/pdf/Final_FREQUENTLY_ASKED_QUESTIONS_-PATENT.pdf accessed 02 December 2020.

or is not available at an affordable price, then the Controller can grant compulsory license.

- Section 86 deals with the power of the Controller to adjourn applications for compulsory licenses. Section 87 deals with the procedure for dealing with applications under Section 84 and Section 85.
- Section 87 deals with the procedure for dealing with applications under Section 84 and Section 85.
- Section 88 deals "with the powers of the Controller in granting compulsory licenses. Section 89 covers the General purposes for granting compulsory licenses and provides that Section 84 be exercised 'with a view to securing general purposes', which means that patented inventions are worked commercially in India 'without undue delay and to the fullest extent that is reasonably practicable'; or that the interests of any person who is working or developing an invention India are not unfairly prejudiced".[6]
- Section 90 enables the Patent Controller to lay down the 'terms and conditions' on which the compulsory license should be issued.
- Section 92 enables the Central Government to issue compulsory license.
- Section 92A enables the government to issue compulsory license to export pharmaceutical products to meet the public health emergency faced by another country.
- Section 93 states that grant of any compulsory license shall operate as a deed executed by the patentee under certain terms and conditions as settled by the Patent Controller.
- Section 94 deals with the termination of compulsory license.

Chapter XXIII deals with 'Miscellaneous,' and Section 140 provides for 'Avoidance' of certain restrictive conditions.

It is also essential to briefly discuss the Competition Act 2002 since the provisions of this Act impact Standard Essential Patents as well. Section 3 of the Competition Act, 2002 deals with anticompetitive agreements, and abuse of dominance is dealt by Section 4. Under the existing Act, Section 3(5) specifically protects the rights under IP or Copyright regime subject to reasonable conditions in cases of anticompetitive agreements. However, a similar protection is not available under Section 4.

The Competition Law Review Committee published its report in 2019 in which it was recommended that in cases of:

abuse of dominance, a defense allowing reasonable conditions and restrictions for protecting IPR may be provided. The Committee stated that since the Competition Act, 2002 explicitly mentions this defense in Section 3(5)(i) for anti-competitive agreements, a specific defense should also be provided in relation to Section 4 to avoid any uncertainty.[7]

---

[6] Ibid.

[7] Ministry of Corporate Affairs, *Competition Law Review Committee (CLRC) Report* (July 2019) <http://www.mca.gov.in/Ministry/pdf/ReportCLRC_14082019.pdf> accessed 02 December 2020.

The Committee stated that this defense should be narrowly construed, in line with international jurisprudence. In line with this recommendation, a defense was included in Section 4A of the Draft Competition (Amendment) Bill, 2020.

2.3   National IPR Policy

The National Intellectual Property Rights (IPR) Policy 2016[8] was adopted on 12th May 2016.[9] In the National IPR Policy, the Union Cabinet stressed upon enhancing the marketability of Indian IPRs and called for greater investments, private sector intervention, research and development efforts, academic insights as well as human capital development by building specific skill sets that are required in all creative and technology-oriented sector. The IPR Policy suggests regulatory amendments such that maximum protection of IPRs can be ensured. The amendments also included administrative restructuring to can reduce compliance cost and make compliance procedure more efficient.

The policy covered seven objectives namely—IPR Awareness: Outreach and Promotion, Generation of IPRs, Legal and Legislative Framework, Administration and Management, Commercialization of IPRs, Enforcement and Adjudication and Human Capital Development.[10] The examination of availability of Standard Essential Patents (SEPs) on fair, reasonable, and non-discriminatory (FRAND) terms is among one of the goals of the National IPR policy.[11]

While the National IPR Policy includes some positive measures to streamline IP-related administrative processes and talks about introducing new measures to bolster IP enforcement, the policy has not been able to offer predictability, clarity and transparency for improved investment and business decisions around IPRs.[12]

---

[8] Department of Industrial Policy and Promotion, *National Intellectual Rights Policy* (May 2016) <https://dipp.gov.in/sites/default/files/national-IPR-Policy2016-14October2020.pdf> accessed 02 December 2020.

[9] Press Information Bureau, 'National IPR Policy' (Press Information Bureau, 27 December 2018, New Delhi) <https://pib.gov.in/Pressreleaseshare.aspx?PRID=1557418> accessed 02 December 2020.

[10] *National Intellectual Rights Policy*, n8.

[11] Ibid.

[12] Bharadwaj and Chawla, n1.

2.4 India's Digital Initiatives

2.4.1 Digital India

Digital India is "an umbrella program that covers multiple Government Ministries and Departments. It weaves together many ideas and thoughts into a single, comprehensive vision so that each of them can be implemented as part of a larger goal".[13] The program focuses on "Digital Infrastructure as a Core Utility to Every Citizen; Governance & Services on Demand and Digital Empowerment of Citizen".[14]

Digital India "aims to provide the much-needed thrust to the nine pillars of growth areas, namely Broadband Highways, Universal Access to Mobile Connectivity, Public Internet Access Program, e-Governance: Reforming Government through Technology, e-Kranti - Electronic Delivery of Services, Information for All, Electronics Manufacturing, IT for Jobs and Early Harvest Program. Each of these areas is a complex program and cuts across multiple Ministries and Departments."[15]

2.4.2 Make in India

As part of the national building initiative, the 'The Make in India' initiative was started in September 2014. With the motto of "Minimum Government, Maximum Governance" the initiative aimed to overhaul the cumbersome processes so that India can tap into its potential and become a global hub for manufacturing and design.

The Make in India is built on collaborative efforts between various departments of the government and business enterprises. This was initiated through the DIPP which coordinated with the various government agencies at the Union and State level and also brought together Union Ministries, industry leaders, and various knowledge partners.

The initiative is designed to "facilitate investment, foster innovation, enhance skill development, protect intellectual property, and build best in class manufacturing infrastructure in the country. The primary objective of this initiative is to attract investments from across the globe and strengthen India's manufacturing sector".[16]

---

[13] Digital India, 'How Digital India will be realized: Pillars of Digital India' https://digitalindia. gov.in/content/programme-pillars (accessed 02 December 2020).

[14] Ibid.

[15] Ibid.

[16] IBEF, *Make in India* https://www.ibef.org/economy/make-in-india (accessed 21 March 2022).

2.5   DIPP Consultation Paper

The Department of Industrial Policy and Promotion issued a consultation paper[17] on Standard Essential Patents and their availability on FRAND terms in March 2016, and sought views and comments of stakeholders. The paper gave an overview and of the concepts of Standards, Standard Essential Patent, patent hold-up, FRAND, patent pooling, and cross-licensing. The Paper also gives an overview of Competition Law issues vis-à-vis Standard Essential Patents and the roles different SSOs play in the standardization process. The judicial approach toward Standard Essential Patents in United States of America, Europe, Japan, and China are also discussed along with an overview of the existing framework for SEP in India. In the most intriguing final section, the Paper offers a lists of issues for resolution. Several responses were received by DIPP, but no final report was released for this consultation paper. The DIPP raised 13 questions around SEPs, which are listed below:

(a)   Whether the existing provisions in the various IPR-related legislations, especially the Patents Act, 1970 and Anti-Trust legislations, are adequate to address the issues related to SEPs and their availability on FRAND terms? If not, then can these issues be addressed through appropriate amendments to such IPR related legislations? If so, what changes should be affected.

(b)   What should be the IPR policy of Indian Standard Setting Organizations in developing Standards for Telecommunication sector and other sectors in India where Standard Essential Patents are used?

(c)   Whether there is a need for prescribing guidelines on working and operation of Standard Setting Organizations by Government of India? If so, what all areas of working of SSOs should they cover?

(d)   Whether there is a need for prescribing guidelines on setting or fixing the royalties in respect of Standard Essential Patents and defining FRAND terms by Government of India? If not, which would be appropriate authority to issue the guidelines and what could be the possible FRAND terms?

(e)   On what basis should the royalty rates in SEPs be decided? Should it be based on Smallest Saleable Patent Practicing Component (SSPPC), or on the net price of the Downstream Product, or some other criterion?

(f)   Whether total payment of royalty in case of various SEPs used in one product should be capped? If so, then should this limit be fixed by Government of India or some other statutory body or left to be decided among the parties?

(g)   Whether the practice of Non-Disclosure Agreements (NDA) leads to misuse of dominant position and is against the FRAND terms?

(h)   What should be the appropriate mode and remedy for settlement of disputes in matters related to SEPs, especially while deciding FRAND terms? Whether injunctions are a suitable remedy in cases pertaining to SEPs and their availability on FRAND terms?

---

[17] Department of Industrial Policy and Promotion, '*Discussion paper on Standard Essential Patents and their Availability on FRAND Terms*' (March 2016) <https://dipp.gov.in/sites/default/files/standardEssentialPaper_01March2016_0.pdf> accessed 02 December 2020.

(i)   What steps can be taken to make the practice of crosslicensing transparent so that royalty rates are fair and reasonable?

(j)   What steps can be taken to make the practice of patent pooling transparent so that royalty rates are fair and reasonable?

(k)   How should it be determined whether a patent declared as SEP is an essential patent, particularly when bouquets of patents are used in one device?

(l)   Whether there is a need of setting up of an independent expert body to determine FRAND terms for SEPs and devising methodology for such purpose?

(m)   If certain standards can be met without infringing any SEP, for instance by use of some alternative technology or because the patent is no longer in force, what should be the process to declassify such a SEP?[18]

2.6   The TRAI Consultation Paper and the Recommendation Papers

The TRAI Consultation Paper and the Recommendation Papers (January and February 2018, respectively)[19] set the foundations for the National Digital Communications Policy (NDCP) 2018 by identifying the goals, scope, and stakeholders for the policy. The two papers are important for they set the foundational tone for the policy by (1) identifying the goals and the stakeholders of the policy, (2) redefining the scope of the policy to keep it in line with its goals, and (3) suggesting the focus areas for the policy accordingly. Post liberalization, the Indian Telecom sector witnessed the influence of four major policies with the following focus areas.

The National Telecom Policy, 1994 was brought about with the vision of providing universal service that connected all villages by year 1997.[20] The New Telecom Policy, 1999 repeated a similar vision of provision of Universal Service that extended to unconnected rural areas with a new deadline of 2002.[21] It envisioned all district-headquarters having Internet access by year 2000. Then in 2004, the Broadband Policy came about recognizing the role of broadband services in multidimensional development of the country and need to lay down the infrastructure facilitating the

---

[18] Ibid.

[19] Telecom Regulation Authority of India, '*Consultation Paper on Inputs for Formulation of National Telecom Policy*' – *2018* (3 January 2018) <https://www.trai.gov.in/sites/default/files/CP_on_NTP_03012018.pdf>; Telecom Regulation Authority of India, *Inputs for Formulation of National Telecom Policy-2018* (2 February 2018) <https://www.trai.gov.in/sites/default/files/Recommendation_NTP_2018_02022018.pdf> accessed 02 December 2020.

[20] Department of Telecommunication, Ministry of Communications, '*National Telecom Policy, 1994*' (Modified on 5 August 2016) <http://dot.gov.in/national-telecom-policy-1994> accessed 02 December 2020.

[21] Department of Telecommunication, Ministry of Communications, '*New Telecom Policy, 1999*' (Modified on 5 August 2016) <http://www.dot.gov.in/new-telecom-policy-1999> accessed 02 December 2020.

same. It estimated the number of Internet subscriptions to reach 40 million and that of broadband to reach 20 million by year 2010.[22]

The next major policy that offered radical changes was the National Telecom Policy, 2012 It came after a substantial gap, but it put forward a vision of bringing about some major transformations in the country. With the primary aim of accelerating economic growth and enhancing the contribution of the telecommunications sector, the Department of Telecommunications (DoT) selected the areas of policy, licensing, and coordination among various forms of communication. It sought for international cooperation in telecommunication matters; promoting standardization and R&D and funding for the same; and aimed at calling in more private investment.[23] Thus, when asked to give suggestions for the 2018 policy, the TRAI began with analyzing thoroughly the 2012 policy first to derive at a concrete, far-reaching strategy for the 2018 Policy. Accordingly, the Consultation Paper, sought suggestions from various stakeholders clearly establishing that the focus shall be on enabling ease of doing business, achieving infrastructural coherence with advances in the fourth Industrial Revolution, and building a strong domestic IPR market that attracts global attention for investment.

One of the early realizations of the stakeholders was that since the policy is bound to affect the entire ICT sector, it was imperative to widen the scope of the policy and the same should be reflected in the title of the Policy too. Thus, propositions were made to change the title from the traditional "National Telecom Policy, 2018" to "National Information and Communication Technology Policy-2018". Another focal point of discussion was the subscription rate in the rural areas, an aim unfulfilled from the previous policy and carried forward to the current one after modifications.

Widening the scope of the policy automatically brought to attention the inevitable need to converge the networks, which would be necessary for efficient utilization of resources. This would require extensive research and development to bring about innovative changes in technology—an issue that was discussed in the consultation meetings. The stakeholders also realized that this kind of digital transformation of country's economy and industry necessitated recognizing telecommunication networks as essential infrastructure in addition to the physical ones. The discussions also emphasized on making telecom services more reliable, prompt, and cost-effective to support other related missions of the Government such as 'Digital India'.

The TRAI consultation meetings also focused on the national vision of having a knowledge-based economy in the country. The discussions drew attention toward the decades old framework for calculating licensing fee and spectrum usage charges, and the danger of "cascading of levies" due to converging nature of the Internet-ways.

---

[22] Department of Telecommunications, Ministry of Communications and Information Technology, *'Broadband Policy', 2004* (Modified on 5 August 2016) <http://dot.gov.in/broadband-policy-2004> accessed 02 December 2020.

[23] Department of Telecommunications, Ministry of Communications and Information Technology, *'National Telecom Policy (NTP) 2012'* <http://dot.gov.in/relatedlinks/national-telecom-policy-2012> accessed 02 December 2020.

Suggestions were also made to streamline multiple pending litigations in matters related to Adjusted Gross Revenue (AGR) in telecom.

To prepare for the fourth Industrial Revolution ahead in time, the TRAI Consultation Paper suggested that the Right of Ways permissions should be granted expeditiously and in a transparent manner. From the revenue perspective, logical suggestions of freeing the infrastructure for non-government use were welcomed. Keeping the consumer interest and data literacy paramount, the Consultation Paper suggests development of data centers for the government telecom schemes to reach the rural and uncovered areas. It emphasized on the potential of the 'Propel India' mission to the possibility of becoming a pioneer in the upcoming Industrial Revolution in consonance with the similarly floated policies of the Government of India like Digital India,[24] Smart Cities Mission,[25] Start-up India[26] and Make in India.[27] The government has aided these objectives by providing for incubation centers, expert guidance, encouraging research and development, and financial aid. To support these plans, the policies also realize the need for developing globally comparable standards and design uniformization and effectuating easy and transparent licensing of the same.

The emphasis on widening the scope of the policy and building a strong, sustainable, coherent, and flexible telecommunications infrastructure comes into an even better perspective when viewed through the lens of the Industrial Policy released by the Department of Industrial Policy and Promotion in 2017. Since liberalization, India's industrial policy focused on certain key elements including abolishing industrial licensing, attracting foreign investment, improving Indian access to advanced technology (mostly foreign technology with limited technology transfer), improving innovative capacity, and to nurture healthy competition among the Indian industries.

While over the years India has made consistent progress in industrial controls and FDI, the industry continues to face challenges in the other areas. These challenges include the problems of inadequate infrastructure the quality of which can match global standards, convoluted and tedious business environment with high compliance costs, slow shift in technology, low levels of productivity, reduced global demand for domestically manufactured products and services, unattended research and development and innovation sector.

---

[24] Ministry of Electronics and Information Technology, '*Digital India: Power to Empower*' <https://www.digitalindia.gov.in/> accessed 02 December 2020.

[25] Ministry of Housing and Urban Affairs, '*Smart Cities Mission*' (25 June 2015) <http://www.smartcities.gov.in/> accessed 02 December 2020.

[26] Department for Promotion of Industry and Internal Trade, Ministry of Commerce and Industry, '*Startup India*' (16 January 2016) <https://www.startupindia.gov.in/> accessed 02 December 2020.

[27] Department for Promotion of Industry and Internal Trade, Ministry of Commerce and Industry, '*Make in India*' (September 2014) <http://www.makeinindia.com/home> accessed 02 December 2020.

2.7   The National Digital Communications Policy

The National Digital Communications Policy (NDCP)[28] was rolled out by the Department of Telecom in May 2018 with the agenda of preparing a digitally connected India for the future. The Policy, while acknowledging the global shift to 5G, aims at achieving widespread, grassroot-level broadband connectivity and suggests laying down the requisite infrastructure. Some of its strategic objectives include—broadband for all, creation of numerous jobs in the Digital Communications sector, enhancing the productivity of the Digital Communications sector by harnessing most efficient and affordable innovation and technology, encouraging Research and Development (R&D), and attracting investment.

The mission strategizes the accomplishment of the objectives through easing the infrastructural limitations in digital communications by according the telecom infrastructure a status of 'Critical and Essential Infrastructure' similar to the railways and roadways. The measures include replacing the existing infrastructure with a more advanced, efficient, and durable systems and equipment; by relaxing the taxes, levies, spectrum usage charges (SUCs), service cost and simplifying compliance obligations to harness investment and innovation; and by creating a roadmap for synergizing emerging technologies in the telecom sector. Being mindful of the ever-changing nature of technology, the Policy takes cognizance of developing such networks, devices and systems that can easily be ported to or can adapt to such advancements, promising a more judicious use of resources. The Policy aims to leverage Artificial Intelligence and Big Data to enhance the quality of service to attract global attention and interest as well as serve domestic needs. It also stresses upon the need for enhancing domestic manufacturing and creating a Preferential Market Access to domestic products and services.

The NDCP 2018, most importantly, places a heavy reliance on an IPR regime that not only incentivises innovation, but is in congruence with the objectives of the National IPR Policy, 2016. This is imperative for this forms the backbone to strengthening domestic participation in international and collaboration standard development processes that are the bedrock of the high-tech digital communication sector. In this context, an ideal IPR regime must be able to bring the Indian IP standards at par with the global standards by facilitating access of essential background IPR to domestic manufacturers and innovators on fair, reasonable, and non-discriminatory (FRAND) terms.

The NDCP 2018 echoes similar objectives as the National IPR Policy 2016 whose vision is to make India scientifically and technologically efficient such that creativity

---

[28] Department of Telecommunications, Ministry of Communication, *National Digital Telecommunications Policy 2018: Draft for Consultation* (1 May 2018) <http://dot.gov.in/sites/default/files/2018%2005%2025%20NDCP%202018%20Draft%20for%20Consultation_0.pdf> accessed 02 December 2020.

and innovation can prosper.[29] Interestingly, there are more than just these many similarities between the objectives of the National IPR Policy and the NDCP. The National IPR Policy emphatically mentions the need to create awareness about the nature of IPR regime that the country needs to adopt, the need to reverse the concerns of right holders toward IPR as well as public's faith in the Intellectual Property for their betterment in the fields of health, food, and environment. Covering the rural and remote areas specifically in this regard is also likely spirited in the policies. Just like the NDCP, the National IPR Policy also stresses upon enhancing the marketability of Indian IPRs and calling for investments, private sector intervention, research and development, academic insight as well as human capital development by building specific skill set required in the sector.

The vision and implementation plan of NDCP 2018 is multi-dimensional and includes three missions—Connect India, Propel India, and Secure India, which are explained below.

2.7.1 Connect India

The Connect India mission fulfills the DoT's vision to meet the Internet-based communication and information needs of all the citizens of the country through a well-laid infrastructure for digital communication. The factors that are emphasized upon in pursuit of this mission are socio-economic imperatives of citizens, quality of service and sustainability of the environment. The aim is to accomplish several goals by year 2022, including providing universal broadband coverage at a minimal desired speed to (a) every user covering all villages, (b) key development institutions, and (c) educational institutions; a fixed line broadband reaching all households; an increased 'unique mobile subscriber density'; widespread deployment of public Wi-Fi Hotspots; and connectivity to all hitherto uncovered areas.

2.7.2 Secure India

The vision delivered by the Secure India mission is to establish a data protection regime that is aligned with the legal framework governing data privacy, autonomy, and choice of individuals. The mission emphasizes safety and standardized security of digital communication where the standards are set in consonance with the global standards arrived at after paying due consideration to our indigenous needs. The mission ensures data sovereignty and principles of net neutrality, while ensuring institutional accountability. The mission also ensures that there is an efficient registry that is fully functional for addressing security, theft, and other data-related issues.

---

[29] Department of Industrial Policy and Promotion, '*National Intellectual Rights Policy*' (May 2016) <https://dipp.gov.in/sites/default/files/national-IPR-Policy2016-14October2020.pdf> accessed 02 December 2020.

One of the most promising goals of the mission is to develop a Public Protection Disaster Relief (PPDR) plan for better preparedness in times of natural disasters.

2.7.3 Propel India

The Propel India mission comes across as the most ambitious but challenging mission of the policy. The primary goals of the mission include calling for a substantial increase in investment by private and foreign entities in the digital communications sector in India. Accordingly, the policy makes plans for making some ambitious legislative and administrative amends to enable the sector to attract investments worth 100 billion USD. The mission elaborates on the need to review the existing regulatory and licensing frameworks and make them friendlier for investment, innovation, start-ups, and research. It also emphasizes on the need to encourage more start-ups in this sector to embrace the IPR regime and contribute towards strengthening it. To prepare India for Industrial Revolution 4.0, the policy aims at creating more skilled manpower, and expanding Internet of Things (IoT) to its wider horizons. It also aims at developing Standard Essential Patents (SEPs) in digital communications technologies to harness the best available technology at affordable rates for maximum digital, social, and economic development.

3 European Union

3.1 Overview of European Patent System

The European Patent Office (EPO) follows a harmonized procedure to accept, examine and grant patents in the European Economic Area. Patents in EU can either be protected through the patents granted by national IP offices of member states or through those granted by the EPO directly. The European Patent Convention (EPC) provides a robust uniform procedure for the grant of European patents. The interface between the national IP offices and the centralised operations of the EPO is based on smooth interaction between European laws and national laws—a technically and procedurally sophisticated system that has been working without concerns or disruptions for several years now.[30]

---

[30] European Patent Office, *'National Law Relating to the EPC'* (October 2019, 20th Edition) < http://documents.epo.org/projects/babylon/eponet.nsf/0/32A79B8E16750D76C12584D5005ABF 91/$File/national_law_relating_to_the_epc_20th_edition_en.pdf> accessed 02 December 2020.

3.2 EU and Standardization

Standardization process enables patent holders to submit their relevant protected technologies to become a part of technical standards. These standards enable innovative technologies to be more readily adopted by all stakeholders and at the same time ensure licensing of these technologies on fair, reasonable, and non-discriminatory basis.[31] Standards are developed by SSOs and the formal SSOs in Europe are the European Committee for Standardization (CEN), the European Committee for Electrochemical Standardization (CENELEC), and the European Telecommunication Standards Institute (ETSI). These SSOs are mandated by the European Commission (EC) to produce standards which are known as European Norms (ENs). Owing to the importance of innovation and standardization, there have been extensive debates on patents and standards in the EU. The following sections cover the important developments relating to standardization in the EU.

3.3 Public Consultation on Patent and Standards

The EC held a 'Public Consultation on Patent and Standards' between October 2014 and February 2015 to discover ways for effective SEP licensing to make the process appealing for both the SEP holder and the standard implementer.[32] The objective of this consultation was "to gather information and views on the interplay between standardization and intellectual property rights (IPR) such as patents."[33] The purpose was to also ensure that the stakeholders who are interested in standardization should take into consideration how the current framework governing standardization involving patents performs how it should evolve to ensure that standardization remains efficient and adapted to the fast-changing economic and technological environment?[34]

The task at hand was to ensure that the working of EU Single Market is efficient, and the standardization system was effective fulfilling EU's objectives of "industry policy, innovation, services and technological development."[35]

---

[31] European Commission, 'Patents and Standards' <ec.europa.eu/growth/industry/policy/intellect ual-property/patents/standards_en> accessed 02 December 2020.

[32] European Commission, Public Consultation on Patents and Standards—A Modern Framework for Standardisation Involving Intellectual Property Rights (2015) <https://ec.europa.eu/growth/con tent/public-consultation-patents-and-standards-modern-framework-standardisation-involving_en> accessed 02 December 2020.

[33] Ibid.

[34] Ibid.

[35] Ibid.

3.4 Setting Out the EU Approach to SEPs

The European Commission published a communication on November 2017 ("EC Communication").[36] The EC Communication facilitates a policy framework that enables wider access and better connectivity to key technological innovations. Smart cities, smart homes, and other such interconnected products have the estimated economic potential of up to €9 trillion by 2025, which is why the EC is determined to drive economic growth through technology advancement. This economic potential was seen as the next force that is going to drive the economic growth in Europe as IoT will drive homes, offices, factories, automobiles, and cities in most parts of the world. The EC aims to position Europe as a leading global player for making such devices provided the patent holders continue to develop technologies that can be declared as standards by SSOs. This is essential from the point of interoperability and wide dissemination, and also from the perspective of committing to giving out licenses that are based on FRAND terms.

Some concerns around SEPs that were identified by the EC necessitated an urgent response so that growth and development of the ICT sector would not stall.[37] The EC Communication identified that implementers who intend to utilize SEPs for integrating their products (vehicles, medical equipment, home appliances, etc.) are not necessarily from the ICT sector, which is predominantly contributing existing and new technologies to the hyper connected world. This is a problem as most of these players may not be fully aware of the licensing practices that existed and matured within the global ICT sector. Existing licensing practices within the ICT sector might be incommensurate with the business interest and practices of the other industrial sectors who will primarily be seeking licenses from SEP holders in the ICT sector.

The EC Communication had already identified that SEP holders in the ICT sectors had pending issues to be discussed and settled with implementers citing delaying tactics during negotiating of licenses. The 'unwillingness' of certain licensees have also compounded the problem of SEP holders by using the underlying technology without seeking licenses. The implementers, on the other hand, complain that SEP holders in the ICT sector tend to lay down conditions and demand royalties that are not based on FRAND terms. Further, the threat of injunctive relief sought by SEP holders forces implementers to accept non-FRAND terms to ensure that they are not stopped from manufacturing and marketing their products. Therefore, the EC Communication was determined to address three major issues:

- lack of transparency in terms of essentiality of SEPs
- lack of clarity in the valuation of patents and understanding as to what constitutes FRAND
- the risk of uncertainty in the enforcement of SEPs.

---

[36] European Commission, 'Setting out the EU Approach to Standard Essential Patents' COM (2017) 712 final <https://ec.europa.eu/docsroom/documents/26583> accessed 02 December 2020.
[37] Ibid.

While it is given that standardizing technologies increases interoperability and allows adopting such technologies by telecommunication and mobile manufacturers, it has always been a matter of grave concern as to what exactly has been subject to standardization. Lack of such information tends to delay negotiations of SEPs. Barring the declaration databases made available by SSOs, there is lack of transparency in terms of relevant patents that are subject to standards. This essentially raises the risks for small and medium enterprises (SMEs) and start-ups, companies having limited market reach and entities that have limited or no experience in dealing with SEPs.

Such entities may not be able to anticipate the extent to which royalties have to be negotiated and to understand the need to separate or not separate essential with non-essential patents. This results in instances where implementers are ignorant of patents that they are infringing. It can also result in mistrust between negotiating parties, which may ultimately frustrate the interests of both parties. Such an environment is neither conducive for the SEP holder nor for the implementers. The EC Communication seeks to address the problem of transparency by outlining a set of measures that could reduce information asymmetry and as such enable faster negotiation of licenses between the parties.

The EC Communication particularly identified that the SSO declarations of standards are not user-friendly especially with start-ups and businesses that are not necessarily associated with the telecommunication sector but are primarily integrating such technologies in other devices or technologies. Another key concern is related to how declarations lack any information as to which of those patents are essential to the declared standard. Improving information about the essential patents to a standard and providing user friendly and accessible information about patented technology that has been declared as a standard, would facilitate faster negotiations, and will increase confidence and trust among implementers. Access to such information could be further enhanced by linking patent information to patent office databases, adding updates about the status of the patents, giving information about transfer of patents and strict scrutiny of the declarations made by patent holders.

Enhanced information about the patents that are essential to a standard would reduce the burden on willing licensees as the current practice requires them to identify essential patents from other patents that are usually associated with a standard. The EC Communication suggested that burden on the implementer can be reduced if an independent party with technical know-how can scrutinize the patents declared as part of a standard and identify essential ones. Further, the EC Communication insisted for the need to updated declarations. This is vital as at the time of declaring standards many patents may not have been granted and might be at the stage of being examined in the patent office or merely a patent application might have been filed.

Updated information can contain grant of patent and any change in the scope of the claims made in the patent applications. This can have significant implications especially if the scope of the claim has been reduced at the time of grant of the patent. Additionally, linking the patents declared in the standard process to patent families can also aid the prospective licensees in scrutinizing the patents. The patents that are part of standards have also been subject to litigations. However, it is important to note that only a few patents associated with a standard are the subject matter of litigation. Any update on the progress of such litigation, and the verdict in such cases that can be easily traced and linked to a particular standard, is especially useful to implementers who may not necessarily be equipped with such information at the time of negotiating licenses.

The EC Communication considers the jurisprudence developed in *Unwired Planet v Huawei* wherein the UK High Court concluded that global licenses may not be anticompetitive or abusive. This is primarily based on the rationale of convenience and efficiency. It would be expensive and time consuming for parties to enter licenses based on each jurisdiction. SEP holder having a large portfolio of licenses would also be similarly inconvenienced if it were to formalize a license based on each SEP. It would be rather practical to enter a global portfolio license unless it amounts to an anticompetitive behavior. The EC Communication further recommended patent pools and cross licensing where possible and if it is within feasible competition norms.

While the EC Communication has undeniably emphasized on the need to increase transparency, it has also acknowledged that the burden should not be disproportionately placed on any one stakeholder. Instead, it has suggested a gradual approach to increase transparency which should begin with new standards declared by SSOs. It has advocated a system wherein SSOs could seek a modest fee from the members and create a system of issuing transparency rating or certification for each newly declared standard.

The Commission paper referred to the intention of setting up an expert group to gather expertise on FRAND licensing. The Expert Group had the mandate to give suggestions related to "licensing and valuation of SEPs".[38] The tasks includes:

a.   to facilitate an exchange of experience and good practice in the field of licensing and valuation of SEPs;
b.   to provide the Commission with the necessary economic, legal, and technical expertise regarding evolving industry practices related to the licensing of SEPs, the sound valuation of intellectual property, and the determination of FRAND licensing terms;
c.   to assist the Commission in the monitoring of SEP licensing markets to inform any policy measures that may be required for ensuring a balanced framework for smooth, efficient, and effective licensing of SEPs; and
d.   to assist the Commission in obtaining information on licensing and valuation practices in accordance with the Communication from the Commission on Setting out the EU approach to SEPs.[39]

The EC Communication has been received very positively by the stakeholders for one reason that it emphasizes the need to strike a balance between various interests

[38] European Commission, *Commission Decision of 5.7.2018 Setting Up a Group of Experts on Licensing and Valuation of Standard Essential Patents* C (2018) 4161 final <http://ec.europa.eu/transparency/regexpert/indexcfm?do=groupDetail.groupDetailDoc&id=37653&no=1> accessed 02 December 2020.
[39] Ibid.

instead of holding one over the other. In this effort, it leaves a scope for flexibility in understanding FRAND terms across jurisdictions where parties are negotiating in good faith. It factors in situations where one of parties might be unwilling to license—instances where the party's behavior flouts the guidelines laid down by the CJEU (the 'behavioral criteria' laid down in the *Huawei* judgment[40]). Two concerns that remain paramount while negotiating licenses are efficiency and diffusion of technology. To expedite the negotiations, the EC Communication also highlights the looming uncertainty in SEP dispute resolution. Therefore, a predictable framework fostering time-adhering dispute resolution can create confidence among investors, reduce risks and benefit all stakeholders. Providing sufficient and relevant information, a concrete and specific counteroffer from the implementer, proportional injunctive relief, fixed security to deter hold-out strategies are a few ways that the EC recognizes as behavior showing willingness to license.[41] The Communication also makes it a point to address the involvement of Patent Assertion Entities (PAEs) and the possibility of anticompetitive behavior thereof and, thus, treats them at par with SEP holders on applicability of rules.

3.5   Standard Essential Patents and the Internet of Things: In-Depth Analysis, European Union

The European Parliament's Committee on Legal Affairs (JURI) commissioned a report titled "EU approach to Standard Essential Patents" which examined the issue of transparency, valuation of SEPs, and enforcement of FRAND encumbered SEPs. The report also examined how FRAND disputes are resolved through various approaches like negotiation, mediation, pools, litigation, etc.[42]

---

[40] *Huawei Technologies Co. Ltd v ZTE Corp* (Case C-170/13) EU:C: 2015:477.

[41] European Commission, '*Commission Decision of 5.7.2018 Setting Up a Group of Experts on Licensing and Valuation of Standard Essential Patents* C (2018) 4161 final' http://ec.europa.eu/transparency/regexpert/index.cfm?do=groupDetail.groupDetailDoc&id=37653&no=1 accessed 02 December 2020.

[42] European Commission, *Standard Essential Patents, and the Internet of Things: In-Depth Analysis, European Union* (January 2019) <http://www.europarl.europa.eu/supporting-analyses> accessed 02 December 2020.

3.6   Guidelines on the Handling of the Antitrust Compulsory License Objection According to Huawei v. ZTE Within the Munich Procedure of Handling Patent Infringement Cases

On February 4, 2020, the Regional Court Munich I published "Guidelines on the handling of the antitrust compulsory license objection according to *Huawei v. ZTE* within the Munich Procedure of Handling Patent Infringement Cases". The Guidelines are not binding, but if the parties to a dispute agree, then the courts can conduct speedy proceeding as contentious issues would have been already dealt with.[43]

3.7   EU Communication Making the Most of the EU's Innovative Potential an Intellectual Property Action Plan to Support the EU's Recovery and Resilience

The "Action Plan on Intellectual Property" aims to enable small and medium-sized companies (SMEs), to benefit from their innovations. The Action Plan seeks to "increase protection for intellectual property, boost the uptake of IP by SMEs, facilitate the sharing of IP, fight counterfeiting and improve enforcement of IP rights, promote a global level playing field".[44]

The Action Plan notes that:

> the licensing of standard-essential patents (SEPs) is often a cumbersome and costly exercise for both patent holders and technology implementers and that there is a need for a much clearer and more predictable framework, incentivizing good faith negotiations rather than recourse to litigation.[45]

In the absence of any guidance from the SEP Communication of 2017, the Plan stated that organizations operating in this industry are facing challenges around licensing of SEPs that are leading to legal disputes between prospective licensors and licensees. The former section of the industry was claiming infringement of their patents, while the latter section was claiming imposition of unfair conditions in licensing.

The Plan provides that in the short term the EC would 'facilitate industry-led initiatives to reduce frictions and litigations among players in specific sectors, and

---

[43] Mathieu Klos, '*New FRAND guidelines published by Munich Regional Court*' (Juve Patent, 4th February 2020) <https://www.juve-patent.com/news-and-stories/legal-commentary/new-frand-gui delines-from-munich-regional-court/> accessed 02 December 2020.

[44] European Commission, '*Making the Most of the EU's Innovative Potential an Intellectual Property Action Plan to Support the EU's Recovery and Resilience*' COM (2020) 760 final <https://ec.eur opa.eu/docsroom/documents/43845/attachments/2/translations/en/renditions/native> accessed 02 December 2020.

[45] Ibid.

consider reforms to further clarify and improve the framework governing SEPs'. Finally, the EC expressed interest in exploring the idea of 'an independent system of third-party essentiality checks in view of improving legal certainty and reducing litigation costs'.[46]

3.8 EU Studies

Over the past decade, several studies have been conducted in the EU in relation to SEPs, standardization and licensing. These studies cover different aspects ranging from FRAND licensing terms, Patent assertion entities to various Landscaping studies. This section will give a brief overview of these studies.

3.8.1 Study on the Interplay Between Standards and Intellectual Property Rights (IPRs)

One of the initial studies conducted in the EU was the study on the Interplay between Standards and Intellectual Property Rights (IPRs), and the report of this study was published in April 2011.[47] The study emphasized that the most important issue that needed to be addressed during the development of standards is the patent in standardized technology. The aim of the study was to conduct quantitative study of the interplay between IPRs and standards and provide updates.

The findings also suggested that "the globalization of actors and the convergence of technologies call for a global perspective on the interplay between IPRs and standardization." The study suggested that the EU policies should promote standardization which is voluntary and led by market and the SSOs should be responsible for the formulation of IPR policies. SSOs IPR policies should be provided with safe harbor from the competition agencies providing flexible business models without resulting into anticompetitive behavior. The study suggested specific solutions to the SSOs. It stated that "clear and binding IPR policies including irrevocable and worldwide licensing commitments; legal certainty in case of the transfer of essential patents to third parties; reasonable incentives for good faith IPR inquiries and disclosure; transparent, complete, and accessible IPR databases; co-operation with patent offices on identifying prior art".[48]

---

[46] Ibid.

[47] Fraunhofer Institute for Communication System, '*Study on the Interplay between Standards and Intellectual Property Rights (IPRs)*' (April 2011) <https://ec.europa.eu/growth/content/study-int erplay-between-standards-and-intellectual-property-rights-ipr-0_en> accessed 02 December 2020.
[48] Ibid.

3.8.2   Patents and Standards: A Modern Framework for IPR-Based Standardisation, Commissioned by the European Commission (2014)

In another report titled 'Patents and Standards: A Modern Framework for IPR-Based Standardization' in 2014,[49] the issue of efficient licensing of IPR is discussed for the diffusion of innovation. The report suggests that this problem is more prevalent in the patents on technologies that are declared as standards and efficient licensing mechanism is essential for the success of the standard. The licensing of such SEPs is exposed to market failures such as "externalities (positive and negative), information problems, market power and free-riding".[50] These market failures create barriers to the effective licensing of the SEPs. This study had an objective to "collect qualitative and quantitative data on IPR-based standardization, with a focus on identifying barriers for efficient licensing of SEPs and on possible solutions to these barriers."[51]

The Report recognizes various issues relating to SEP licensing and their respective solutions without affecting the position of EU in the competitive market. This could be achieved by creating a balance between the incentives for investing in an innovation and the economy. There were various issues which arose in the licensing of SEPs such as "information problems, market power and free-riding."[52] Finding solutions to these problems would lead to an efficient licensing of SEPs. This study laid down following possibilities for bringing improvement to the current system:

- Improvements to the patent declaration system
- Promotion of patent pools
- Providing efficient dispute resolution mechanisms
- Clarifying FRAND royalty rate and royalty base
- Transfer of SEP ownership
- Improved guidance on inclusion of patented technologies.

3.8.3   Fair, Reasonable and Non-discriminatory (FRAND) Licensing Terms: Research Analysis of a Controversial Concept, JRC Study (2015)

The principles of licensing under FRAND terms dictate the balancing of interests of diverse stakeholders involved in the process of technical standardization. The primary issue of contention and flux is that the practices that govern licensing on FRAND terms were not systematic. The Joint Research Centre (JRC) is the European Commission's science and knowledge service that provides scientific evidence throughout

---

[49] R N A Bekkers et al., '*Patents and Standards: A Modern Framework for IPR-Based Standardisatio n*' (European Commission, 2014) <https://doi.org/10.2769/90861> accessed 02 December 2020.

[50] Ibid.

[51] Ibid.

[52] Ibid.

the whole policy cycle. The purpose of this JRC Report[53] was "to provide a balanced account of the controversy relating to the FRAND licensing of standard essential patents and to explore future research topics in this area".[54] The JRC Report presents the economic underpinnings of the technical standards in communication, role of the Standard Setting Organizations, and the contribution of FRAND licensing in enabling development and implementation of standards. The Report acknowledges the evolution of licensing practices and the "current controversies on the interpretation of the FRAND licensing principles".[55]

3.8.4 Patent Assertion Entities in Europe: Their Impact on Innovation and Knowledge Transfer in ICT Markets, JRC Study (2016)

'Patent Assertion Entities in Europe',[56] a study on Patent Assertion entities (PAEs) in the EU, examines the impact of their conduct on innovation in the ICT market in EU. The report focused on the business practices of PAEs and its impact on the technology transfer in the ICT sector.[57]

3.8.5 Landscaping Study of Standard Essential Patents, Commissioned by the European Commission (2016)

Another study on publicly-available worldwide-declared SEPs titled *Landscaping Study on Standard Essential Patents (SEPs)* was conducted in the EU.[58] In this study the SEPs were analyzed "to provide a more transparent understanding on the technological concentration and the regional application of SEPs, an overview of global SEP owners as well as an analysis on activities connected to patent licensing, patent trade, patent litigation and patent essentiality."[59] The results of this report were differentiated by SSPs, standards projects, or classification of technology. The report indicated that the SEPs from companies existing in China and Korea are increasing which highlighted the development of the markets in Asia and their importance in the global market.

---

[53] Yann Ménière & Nikolaus Thumm, '*Fair, Reasonable and Non-Discriminatory (FRAND) Licensing Terms*' (Publications Office of the European Union, 2015) <https://publications.jrc.ec.europa.eu/repository/bitstream/JRC96258/jrc96258.pdf> accessed 02 December 2020.

[54] Ibid.

[55] Ibid.

[56] Nikolaus Thumm & Garry Gabison (eds), '*Patent Assertion Entities in Europe*' (Publications Office of the European Union 2016) <http://publications.jrc.ec.europa.eu/repository/handle/JRC103321> accessed 02 December 2020.

[57] Ibid.

[58] IPLYTICS for the European Commission, '*Landscaping Study on Standard Essential Patents (SEP s)*' (2016) <https://ec.europa.eu/growth/content/landscaping-study-standard-essential-patents-europe-0_en> accessed 02 December 2020.

[59] Ibid.

The study also revealed that regional patent offices often exist in the technologically driven areas. By comparing the different SEP portfolios of different patent owners, the study found out varied characteristics in these portfolios. The variations are connected "to the age of the patent portfolio, the regional application as well as to the technological relevance of the patent families."[60] The commitments during the licensing process depend on the respective SSOs and on the technological focus of the standard. License to an SEP is not necessarily required by the SSOs, either the members are not required to enter a license, or they are required to enter one based on default commitments.

3.8.6   Transparency, Predictability and Efficiency of SSO-Based Standardisation and SEP Licensing, CRA Study (2016)

"Transparency, Predictability, and Efficiency of SSO-based Standardization and SEP Licensing", a study conducted to analyze issues that arise during the standardization process, proposed several options to minimize such issues.[61] The issues considered in this study were "lack of clear rules and procedures on the inclusion of patented technologies; problems related to declaration systems; problems related to transfer rules; problems related to patent pools; problems related to FRAND definition; problems related to Dispute resolution".[62]

The objective was not to find a "one-size-fits-all" solution to the identified problems but to provide solutions depending on specific sectors. As a result, a new policy proposal was made that included new analysis-based principles.

3.8.7   Licensing Terms of Standard Essential Patents: A Comprehensive Analysis of Cases, JRC Study (2017)

"Licensing Terms of SEPs" focused on the issues involved in the interpretation of the term FRAND as well as the definition of FRAND royalties.[63] The study provides an analysis of all the cases to provide an understanding of the term FRAND and its varied interpretations.[64] After comparing the different relevant case studies, the study reached the following:

---

[60] Ibid.

[61] Pierre Regibeau, Raphael De Coninck & Hans Zenger, '*Transparency, Predictability, and Efficiency of SSO Based Standardization and SEP Licensing Report for European Commission*' (2016) <https://ec.europa.eu/growth/content/study-transparency-predictability-and-efficiency-sso based-standardization-and-sep-0_en> accessed 02 December 2020.

[62] Ibid.

[63] Chryssoula Pentheroudakis & Justus A Baron, '*Licensing Terms of Standard Essential Patents*' (JRC Science for Policy Report 2017) <https://doi.org/10.2791/32230> accessed 02 December 2020.

[64] Ibid.

1. Idiosyncrasies of SEP litigation
2. Incentive compatibility and fair balance of interests
3. Converging practice on injunctions
4. Evaluation of conduct v. emphasis on royalty rates
5. Core principles of FRAND
6. Methodologies for calculating the FRAND royalty.

The study highlighted that there was no specific methodology to identify a fixed value under FRAND licensing commitment. Determining a FRAND value is very challenging, and it is difficult to give it a 'one-size-fits-all' definition. It varies with sectors, and there are several methods to identify a reasonable rate that follows the FRAND principles. Comparison between the determination of a FRAND rate in USA and Europe has also been drawn in this study which suggests that it is not necessary that methodologies adopted in USA would apply in the European context.

3.8.8 Landscape Study of Potentially Essential Patents Disclosed to ETSI, JRC Study (2020)

This study on potentially essential patents disclosed to the European Telecommunications Standards Institute (ETSI) is a companion to the pilot project on essentiality checks of SEPs. The primary objectives of this research report[65] are to present a landscape analysis of patents that were disclosed to the SDO, the implications for meeting the technical tests of essentiality, and determining differences in quality (technical and economic) of the disclosed patents vis-à-vis comparable but undisclosed patents. The study relied on self-reported data from patentees on patents that "may be or may become essential to an ETSI standard".[66]

The study claimed that "it is a non-trivial task to identify patents from an SDO disclosure database and clean/harmonize/select/de-duplicate/transform that data into information to be used for a given purpose, such as input for a process of essentiality assessment".[67] It shed light on the reporting of patents at SDOs by companies on the belief that they "may be or may become essential". It was observed that the patents disclosed to the ETSI can be considered as the first step in the process to assess the essentiality of patents. One of the findings of the analysis was a "strong upward trend in the number of new patent families being disclosed and that there is considerable fragmentation in the distribution of companies that disclosed these patents, and that the distribution is skewed".[68] Another important finding was that given the current state of disclosures and the technicalities involved, though seemingly desirable, it is

---

[65] Rudi Bekkers, et al., 'Landscape Study of Potentially Essential Patents Disclosed to ETSI' (Publications Office of the European Union 2020) <https://publications.jrc.ec.europa.eu/repository/bitstream/JRC115004/> accessed 02 December 2020.

[66] Pentheroudakis and Baron, n63.

[67] Ibid.

[68] Ibid.

not practical to accurately break down the ETSI disclosures in cellular wireless standards. Finally, the study pointed to a higher quality in technical merit and economic value (as empirically determined by commonly used proxies) of disclosed essential patents compared to non-disclosed patents in the same patent classifications.

3.8.9 Pilot Study for Essentiality Assessment of Standard Essential Patents, Joint Research Centre (JRC) Study (2020)

This aim of this study was to investigate the "technical and institutional feasibility of a system that ensures better essentiality scrutiny for Standard Essential Patents (SEPs)".[69] While making the following recommendations, the report broadly concluded that transparent data on essentiality is beneficial for all stakeholders.

(a)   For the purposes of defining procedures, designing the system, overseeing the process and harmonizing it with international systems, the EC should arrange for a supervisory body with the responsibility of assuring quality and performance.

(b)   A detailed assessment procedure developed in the pilot experiment be used as input when specifying and designing a system was recommended.

(c)   Training and validating AI systems for specific tasks was recommended in the report.

(d)   Patent owners and implementers must consider how a system for essentiality assessments can benefit them respectively, and how they can support such a system.

(e)   The European Patent Office, national patent offices and/or patent organizations must take into consideration the recommendation of carrying out essentiality assessments proactively.

(f)   It was recommended that patent pools along with their members investigate the ongoing and finished assessments as a precursor to the essentiality assessment system, and engage with the EC to discuss implementation of a fast-track procedure.

(g)   Patent pools along with their members must undertake investigation of whether "the essentiality assessments under the new system can play a role in their own patent inclusions procedures".[70]

(h)   SDOs must execute recommendations for improving the rules and processes governing disclosures and for enabling access to data on disclosure.

---

[69] Ibid.

[70] Ibid.

4   United States of America (USA)

Technology innovation has historically played a vital role in the economy of the United States America. Innovation has fueled the rapid pace of economic growth during the First Industrial Revolution and, in recent times, also benefitted consumers as new innovative products brought about significant enhancements in the lives of people. The U.S. government acknowledged that nearly 45 million are directly employed by the high-tech industry and the sector has generated more than $6 trillion dollars.[71] While the country's Courts and executive agencies agree on the importance of patent rights, they differ on the remedies that are available when patents are infringed.[72] This section will discuss the views of the executive agencies and the various policies that have been introduced in the country and the views of the USA's Courts shall be discussed in a later part of this book.

4.1   Overview of US Patent System

The US Constitution states that the Congress has the power to "… [t]o promote the Progress of Science and useful Arts, by securing for limited Times to Authors and Inventors the exclusive Right to their respective Writings and Discoveries".[73]

The US Congress promulgated the Patent Act, Title 35 of the United States Code (35 U.S.C. §101 et seq.). The Congress has established USPTO as an administrative agency that has evolved rules to implement and enforce the Patent Act.[74]

4.2   USA—Competition Enforcers and Licensing

Licensing of patented technologies not only enables the patent holder to earn revenue but also serves as a means to diffuse innovations. However, restrictive licensing practices that imposes onerous obligations on the licensee or refusal to give licenses can impede fair competition.[75] While a free market is essential to enhance the welfare of the consumers, it is also widely accepted in US that there is a need to allow the

---

[71] OECD, '*Licensing of IP Rights and Competition Law – Note by the United States*' <https://one.oecd.org/document/DAF/COMP/WD(2019)58/en/pdf> accessed 02 December 2020.

[72] Steven Seidenberg, '*US Perspectives: United States Confounded by Standard-Essential Patents*' (*I ntellectual Property Watch*, 29 July 2013) <http://www.ip-watch.org/2013/07/29/us-confounded-by-standard-essential-patents/> accessed 02 December 2020.

[73] U.S. Constitution, Article I, Section 8, Clause 8.

[74] Rules are enshrined in Title 37 of the Code of Federal Regulations (37 C.F.R. §1.1 et seq). *See* A Murphy, et al., '*Introduction to Intellectual Property: A U.S. Perspective*' (2015) 5 Cold Spring Harb Perspect Med. 8.

[75] OECD, '*Licensing of IP Rights and Competition Law*' <https://one.oecd.org/document/DAF/COMP(2019)3/en/pdf> accessed 02 December 2020.

patent ecosystem to thrive in order to disseminate new technologies. It is widely believed in US that patents and fair competition complement each other and as such federal agencies do not impose liability for mere refusal to license or to provide license at a certain royalty rate.[76]

4.3   The 2017 Antitrust Guidelines for the Licensing of Intellectual Property

The Federal Trade Commission (FTC) and the Antitrust Division of the US Department of Justice (DOJ) updated the "Antitrust Guidelines for the Licensing of Intellectual Property" (the Guidelines).[77] The guidelines require the Agencies to follow the three general principles;

> the Agencies should apply the same analysis to conduct involving IP as to conduct involving other forms of property, considering the specific characteristics of a particular property right; the Agencies should not presume that intellectual property creates market power in antitrust context and; the Agencies recognize that the intellectual property licensing allows firms to combine complementary factors of production and is generally pro-competitive.[78]

The Guidelines provide that the agencies analytical framework and enforcement policies with regards to licensing of IP are like the terms as in 1995, with moderate adjustments for developments in law and enforcement policy. The Guidelines did not provide much guidance on the controversial issues emerging out of intersection of IP and antitrust such as issues involving SEPs, Patent Assertion Entities (PAEs), and reverse payment settlements. The Guidelines, however, incorporated the Supreme Court rulings in the agency.

The Guidelines clarified that a "unilateral refusal to assist competitors generally does not result in antitrust liability and a resale price management agreement are not per se illegal and are evaluated under the result in antitrust liability".[79]

---

[76] IP Antitrust Guidelines, s 2.1 ("The antitrust laws generally do not impose liability upon a firm for a unilateral refusal to assist its competitors, in part because doing so may undermine incentives for investment and innovation"); IP Antitrust Report, 6.

[77] U.S. Department of Justice and the Federal Trade Commission, 'Antitrust Guidelines for the Licensing of Intellectual Property' <https://www.justice.gov/atr/IPguidelines/download> accessed 02 December 2020.

[78] Ibid.

[79] Ibid.

4.4 The New Madison Approach

The stricter patent eligibility standards upheld by both, the U.S. courts and the USPTO,[80] in addition to the cautious approach adopted by the SSOs in response to patent-holdups, have discouraged the tech companies, innovators, and investors from spending more on patents in the US and instead secure their product patents in other jurisdictions. As a result, the AAG of the US DoJ, Antitrust Division, Makan Delrahim, in his December 2017 remarks, "Telegraph Road",[81] decided to remedy the deteriorating patent regime in the US by withdrawing its support from the 2013 joint statement with the USPTO entitled "Policy Statement on Remedies for Standards-Essential Patents Subject to Voluntary F/RAND Commitments".[82] The new policy announced a pivot toward taking into account actions of all stakeholders including the holders of the SEPs, the SDOs and the implementers of the standards to examine anticompetitive practices that may or may warrant formal scrutiny by the DoJ. This policy promised to make available injunctive relief to the SEP holder by enforcing the right to exclude under the basic tenets of property law, and without the intervention of the SSO. Additionally, the policy also focuses on civil and contractual remedies rather than antitrust law.

The DoJ, under the new leadership, observed that involving antitrust agencies in disputes related to high-tech SEPs is rather unwarranted and other remedies should be sought to preserve interests of parties in the litigation. For this, emphasis is laid on the contractual nature of the relationship between the holder and the implementer of essential patents that require seeking remedies under contract law. Under common law, when contracts are reneged or contractual obligations are breached by any party, seeking damages and injunctive relief takes primacy over antitrust remedies. According to the new policy, this approach better serves the interests of the litigating parties without interference of the regulatory agencies, and is in sharp contrast to the earlier stand of the DoJ where antitrust investigation was deemed necessary in investigating FRAND commitment to judge the actions of SEP holders.[83] This approach is said to promote competition and innovation. In instances where collusion or any other anticompetitive activities or actions by prospective licensees are explicitly found, intervention by the antitrust agencies is called for.

The remarks of Makan Delrahim rekindled the theory that regulation of private contracts under public law induce distortions in the market such as less than optimal

---

[80] Adam Mossoff & Kevin R. Madigan, 'Turning Gold to Lead: How Patent Eligibility Doctrine is Undermining U.S. Leadership in Innovation', George Mason University Law & Economics Research Paper Series 17-16.

[81] Makan Delrahim, AAG, Antitrust Division (US DoJ), 'Telegraph Road: Incentivising Innovation at the Intersection of Patent and Antitrust Law', December 7, 2018, the 19th Annual Berkeley-Stanford Advanced Patent Law Institute.

[82] United States Depart of Justice and United States Patent and Trademark Office, 'Policy Statement on Remedies for Standards-Essential Patents Subject to Voluntary F/RAND Commitments', January 8, 2013.

[83] Dell Computer Corp. (1996) 121 F.T.C. 616; Union Oil Co. of Cal. (2005) 140 F.T.C. 123; Rambus Inc. (2006) 142 F.T.C. 98.

level of investments or, in some cases, 'patent hold-out'. The intervention of enforce-ment agencies needs to be "exercised with humility" to minimize perverse outcomes in the market. The ambit of the antitrust law could be broadened to include "non-competition public interest factors that balance competition and non-competition factors with equity."[84] It can also be inferred from the multiple speeches delivered by the AAG that the new policy proposal lends support for the self-regulation of SSOs under a dynamic free-market framework. A precautionary, self-regulating approach of the SSOs where internal rules governing patents are weighed alongside antitrust laws would facilitate the standard development process without intervention of the regulatory agencies.

This revitalized approach lays emphasis on the 'symmetric nature of patent hold-up and patent hold-out', which is a recurring issue in most of the AAGs speeches. Several thought-provoking issues arise. If implemented, it may expand the scope of the potential antitrust investigation and, at the same time, bring about a balance to an otherwise complicated yet evolving discourse on the subject. The policy proposed that certain actions of the standard implementers including delays in the licensing process that are not justified or caused due to lack of timely response to negotiation offers can also come under the scanner.

In a speech delivered in China, Delrahim drew attention to a strong belief that under the innovation ecosystem in the US, intellectual property rights belong to the inventor as much as they are for the public. A "new Madison approach" was quoted by the AAG after James Madison who is believed to be the founding father of patent law of the United States.[85]

The premise of the new Madison approach, which forms the basis of Delrahim's arguments, is that the innovation environment will thrive when the incentives to innovate are sufficiently preserved including the inalienable right of the patent holder (SEP holder) to legally exclude others.[86] In the context of patent licensing disputes, when private contracts go under scrutiny by the competition agencies, it may lead to an adverse impact on innovation and market competition.[87] According to the UD DoJ, this is why the use of antitrust law to address problem of patent hold-up is misplaced. In a speech delivered in February 2018 at the College of Europe in Brussels, the AAG articulated the following:

> First, the application of antitrust laws to the issue of hold-up has, so far, remained devoid of empirical data, and therefore, an evidence-based enforcement of antitrust is called for.

---

[84] Koren W. Wong-Ervin, '*Protecting Intellectual Property Rights Abroad: Due Process, Public Interest Factors, and Extra-Jurisdictional Remedies*' George Mason University Law and Economics Research Paper Series 17-18.

[85] Makan Delrahim, Assistant Attorney General, Antitrust Division, US Department of Justice, '*The "New Madison" Approach to Antitrust and Intellectual Property Law*' (speech delivered at University of Pennsylvania Law School, Philadelphia, 16 March 2018).

[86] Makan Delrahim, Assistant Attorney General, Antitrust Division, US Department of Justice, '*Good Times, Bad Times, Trust Will Take Us Far: Competition Enforcement and the Relationship Between Washington and Brussels*' (speech delivered at College of Europe, Brussels, 21 February 2018) 4.

[87] Ibid.

Second, the antitrust law enforcement bodies should ensure that their actions do not transform a private voluntary licensing regime for SEPs into a regime of compulsory licensing. Third, in line with the Madison approach, it is important to look at regulation of SSOs to deter any possibility of collusive behaviour.[88]

The antitrust agencies note the productive role in promoting technology-led innovation that is played by the standard setting organizations despite the existence of a real risk of collusion and anticompetitive behavior in the process of collaborative standard setting. A vital role of the SSOs, therefore, is to balance the interests of different agents that have divergent interests and commercial stakes involved by formulating internal policies governing the use of intellectual property rights. Evolution of standards to keep pace with technological advances require revisiting and revising these IPR policies from time to time. Some of these changes have received a lot of necessary, and sometimes unnecessary, media attention with allegations that they will or may delay the pace of technological progress generally and hinder the time-tested process of technical standard development more specifically. Consensus on the last set of proposed revisions and the revision that were implemented is still lacking.

The views of the AAG Delrahim on the new policy on IPRs in November 2017 echoed the views on the need to preserve rights of innovators for non-stop technological innovation for the benefit of the society. In a speech in November 2017, he stated that the "competition authority must exercise greater humility in the application of antitrust laws to SEPs."[89] After six months, he delivered another power-packed speech enunciating his ideas on antitrust enforcement in the digital era.[90] He said that:

> the antitrust consensus, in my view, has two key components. The first component is the consumer welfare standard, which condemns practices as unlawful where they harm competition in such a way that consumers suffer. The consumer welfare standard is the lodestar of antitrust enforcement, and a humble recognition that antitrust law, if misapplied, can have harmful consequences for those it intends to protect. The second component—which is the focus of my remarks today—is what I and others call "evidence-based enforcement."[91]

Soon after that he responded to a letter written by a group of antitrust and IP law experts supporting an evidence-based approach. He stated that:

> though we are not able to comment on any pending investigations or evidence that we have reviewed, the policies of the United States reflect our observations and understanding of, among other things, actual standard setting activity, actions of participants in SSOs (including

---

[88] Ibid.

[89] Makan Delrahim, Assistant Attorney General, Antitrust Division, US Department of Justice, 'Take It to the Limit: Respecting Innovation Incentives in the Application of Antitrust Law' (speech delivered at USC Gould School of Law, California, 10 November 2017) 10.

[90] Makan Delrahim, Assistant Attorney General, Antitrust Division, US Department of Justice, 'Don't Stop Believin': Antitrust Enforcement in the Digital Era' (speech delivered at the University of Chicago's Antitrust and Competition Conference, Department of Justice, Chicago, 19 April 2018) <https://www.justice.gov/opa/speech/assistant-attorney-general-makan-delrahim-delivers-keynote-address-university-chicagos> accessed 02 December 2020.

[91] Ibid.

both patent holders and implementers), the current state of theoretical and empirical research into these matters, and, of course, the status of patent rights under the US Constitution.[92]

4.5 Policy Statement of Remedies for Standards-Essential Patents Subject to Voluntary F/RAND Commitments

In 2019, the DoJ took a major step withdrawing from the 2013 Joint Policy Statement between DoJ and PTO concerning Remedies for Standard Essential Patents Subject to Voluntary FRAND Commitments listing out several problems in the FRAND licensing process that disincentives innovation.[93] In a continuing process of 'promoting technological innovation, furthering consumer choice and enabling industry competitiveness', the DoJ, the USPTO and the National Institute of Standards and Technology (NIST) released a joint statement on the 19th of December, 2019.[94] The policy statement clarifies the apparent misinterpretation of the 2013 Policy and says that while the inquiry into the F/RAND commitment of the patent holder is relevant, it does not necessarily bar its access to a particular remedy.

While extending the burden of good faith negotiations to both, SEP holders and the potential licensees, the Policy emphatically provides for all kinds of remedies against patent infringement including "reasonable royalties, lost profits, enhanced damages for willful infringement and exclusion orders issues by the U.S. International Trade Commission" as the case at hand may warrant. The Policy also clarifies that when it comes to issues like injunctions and damages, there need not be a special standard for SEPs and the courts can do with the *eBay*[95] standard itself, although given the circumstances of a case, additional factors may be taken into consideration. The Policy leaves the courts to their faculties for making this "balanced, fact-based analysis" to decide upon infringement remedies when the SEPs have been licensed as per the F/RAND commitment under the general laws.

4.6 Business Review Letters (BRL)

There is a 'business review procedure' under the DoJ that allows an organization to propose to the antitrust division acting against a decision or activity. Based on the information furnished, the organization may also request to receive a statement

---

[92] Makan Delrahim, Assistant Attorney General, Antitrust Division, US Department of Justice, <https://www.competitionpolicyinternational.com/wp-content/uploads/2018/05/2018-05-18-Delrahim-Letter-to-Carrier-and-Muris1.pdf> accessed 02 December 2020.

[93] Delrahim, n88.

[94] DoJ, USPTO and NIST, '*Policy statement of Remedies for Standards-Essential Patents Subject to Voluntary F/RAND Commitments*' (19th December 2019) <https://www.uspto.gov/sites/default/files/documents/SEP%20policy%20statement%20signed.pdf> accessed 02 December 2020.

[95] *eBay Inc.*, 547 U.S. at 391–393.

clarifying whether the division intends to legally challenge the action. To better understand this process, it is essential here to discuss a few of the Business Review Letters issued by the Antitrust Division of the US Department of Justice and the updates thereto in relation to SEPs. In this section we will be discussing the Business Letter Review (BLR) of the GSM Association (GSMA), Avanci LLC, and the Institute of Electrical and Electronics Engineers (IEEE).

4.6.1 The Global System for Mobile Communications Association (GSMA)

The GSM Association (GSMA)[96] consisting of mobile network operators issued a BLR in November 2019 which notified the changes to the aspects governing standard setting once the investigation is concluded by the DOJ. The Antitrust Division noted that GSMA had used industry influence in developing eSIMs technology standards.[97] In response, the GSMA developed a new set of standard setting procedures that would incorporate inputs from non-members. The BRL issued by GSMA intended to adopt the procedures to which the Antitrust Division expressed certain reservations. According to the DoJ;

> those design limitations ran the risk of limiting the role that an innovative new technology—the embedded SIM (eSIM)—could play in encouraging disruptive competition in the market for mobile wireless service. And by adopting changes to its standard setting procedures before promulgating a new design standard for an interoperable eSIM, the GSMA reduced the risk of an anticompetitive outcome.[98]

The Antitrust Division stated that it was in agreement with the proposed changes made by GSMA.

4.6.2 Avanci LLC

Avanci LLC's new platform for licensing 5G telecommunication technology in the automotive industry resulted in the issuing of BLR by the Antitrust Division. The DOJ had conducted interviews of component supplier in the automotive industry and collected information about the patent pools operating in the sector. The BLR stated that:

> "Avanci's 5G Platform may make licensing standard essential patents related to vehicle connectivity more efficient by providing automakers with a one-stop-shop" for licensing 5G

---

[96] U.S. Department of Justice Antitrust Division, '*Re: GSMA Business Review Letter Request*' <https://www.justice.gov/opa/press-release/file/1221181/download>.

[97] U.S. Department of Justice Antitrust Division, '*Justice Department Issues Business Review Letter to the GSMA Related to Innovative eSIMs Standard for Mobile Devices*' <justice.gov/opa/pr/justice-department-issues-business-review-letter-gsma-related-innovative-esims-standard>.

[98] U.S. Department of Justice Antitrust Division, '*Update 2020*' <https://www.justice.gov/file/128 0196/download>.

technology. The Division concluded that the platform also has the potential to reduce patent infringement and ensure that patent owners who have made significant contributions to the development of 5G specifications are compensated for their innovation. Avanci represented that the Platform will charge FRAND rates for the patented technologies, with input from both licensors and licensees.[99]

The DoJ concluded that Avanci's 5G platform licensing was in compliance with the competition norms.

4.6.3   The Institute of Electrical and Electronics Engineers (IEEE)

The year 2015 witnessed landmark developments that changed the discourse on IP and standard setting when the IEEE announced the adoption of new policy changes on patent licensing in IEEE including grounds to seek injunctive relief, commitments expected from patent holders, and decision regarding arbitration proceedings in licensing disputes. These IEEE rules were developed to ensure that the standard setting activity was guided by minimum procedural safeguard.[100] According to the Standards Board Bylaws of the IEEE-SA, "the standards development stage which included the proposal to standardize, approval of a standard, defining the technical conditions of the standard etc. are guided by openness, due process, balance and right of appeal."[101]

The Division issued a BLR to the IEEE stating that:

> the policy update had the potential to benefit competition and consumers by facilitating licensing negotiations, mitigating hold up and royalty stacking, and promoting competition among technologies for inclusion in standards. The BLR stated that per the Division, the Update's potential pro-competitive benefits were likely to outweigh any anti-competitive harms arising from the policy.[102]

In essence, the revised patent policy of the IEEE turned out to be the first set of regulations in the world by a standard body specifically for FRAND royalties. Since the landmark Rambus decision, courts in the US have almost strictly enforced commitments of paying royalties that are fair, reasonable, and non-discriminatory

---

[99] U.S. Department of Justice, 'Justice Department Issues Business Review Letter to Avanci for Proposed Licensing Platform to Advance 5G Technology for Interconnected Automobiles' <https://www.justice.gov/opa/pr/justice-department-issues-business-review-letter-avanci-proposed-licensing-platform-advance> accessed 02 December 2020.

[100] Nicolo Zingales & Olia Kanevskaia, 'The IEEE-SA Patent Policy Update Under the lens of EU Competition La w' (2016) 12(2–3) European Competition Journal 195.

[101] Standards Board Bylaws, art 2.1, art 5.3.3, 'IEEE-SA Standards Board Operations Manual' (IEEE-SA, December 2015) <http://standards.ieee.org/develop/policies/opman/sb_om.pdf> accessed 02 December 2020.

[102] U.S. Dept. of Justice, '2015 IEEE Business Review Letter' <https://www.justice.gov/file/131 5431/download> accessed 02 December 2020.

to counter opportunism by the licensing parties.[103] The policy changes had a fore-seeable impact on the royalty rates being demanded, the ability to enforce essential patents, and the remedy that SEP holders can seek if patents are infringed. It has been argued elsewhere that "the antitrust division, applauding the efforts of the IEEE, entirely ignored the possible effects of these amendments that may potentially facilitate collusion among implementers."[104]

The Antitrust Division recently notified a supplement[105] to the 2015 letter to IEEE in response to the concerns about the misinterpretation of the 2015 letter that it endorsed patent policy of IEEE. Further, the 2015 letter was outdated in the wake of the new jurisprudence laid out by the courts and also new policy developments that were introduced after 2015. The Division stated that "the 2015 IEEE Letter had proven outdated and that the division feared that reliance on its analysis, both in the United States and abroad, could harm competition and chill innovation".[106]

5 China

5.1 Overview of Chinese IP System

The Patent Law of the People's Republic of China 1984 was amended in 2020. The Patent Amendment sought to increase the patent damages that can be claimed, extended the duration of the design patent term, and introduced the patent term extension.[107] For the enhancement of the existing IP system and actively responding to the international challenges, a National Intellectual Property Strategy was formulated and implemented by the State Council of China. In 2005, National Intellectual Property Strategy Formulation Leading Group was established, and the work related to formulation of the strategy was launched. An outline of the strategy that was released in May 2007 received approval from the Standing Committee of the State Council in April 2008. This made way to the release of the Compendium of China National Intellectual Property Strategy. The State Intellectual Property Office (SIPO) of China explained the significance of the strategy by saying that "China's goal is to become a country with a comparatively high level of intellectual property rights with regard

---

[103] *Ericsson, Inc. v D-Link System, Inc.* (2014) Federal Circuit, 773 F.3d 1201, 1231; *Microsoft Corp. v Motorola, Inc.* (2015) 9th Circuit, 795 F.3d 1024, 1033 citing *Microsoft Corp. v Motorola, Inc.* (2013) Western District of Washington, No. 11 C 9308, 2013 WL 2111217, para 2.

[104] Ashish Bharadwaj & Manveen Singh, '*A Single Spark Can Start A Prairie Fire: Implica tions of the 2015 Amendments to IEEE-SA's Patent Policy*' (2018) 46(1) Capital University Law Review Vol. 46, Issue 4, 2018.

[105] U.S. Department of Justice, '*Updated Response to Electrical and Electronics Engineers Business Review Letter*' <https://www.justice.gov/atr/page/file/1315291/download> accessed 02 December 2020.

[106] Ibid.

[107] Text of China's Amended Patent Law, National Law Review, Volume X, Number 293.

to creation, utilization, protection, and administration by 2020." The main elements
of the strategy have been divided into four sections:

1. Strategic goals: the goal of making China an innovation-led economy with high
    level of IP creation, utilization, protection, and administration by 2020.
2. Guiding principles: the principles being "innovation encouragement, effi-
    cient utilization, lawful protection, and scientific administration". "Innovation
    encouragement" aims at generating numerous independent IPRs in the country.
    "Efficient utilization" refers to the complete exploitation of the true market value
    of its IP. "Lawful protection" implies the need to regulate the abuse of IPR with
    the help of legal enforcement that is not only efficient but effective and rigorous.
    "Scientific administration" refers to the enhancement of the mechanisms to the
    upgrade the efficiency.
3. Strategic focuses: the main aim of the strategy is the improvement of the IP
    system. To fulfill this goal revisions of IP laws and regulations are required
    keeping in mind the national situation of the country. Another aim is to fulfill
    the international obligations of China, alongside strengthening enforcement of
    IP law, tightening systems of administration, and improving IP's guiding role
    in drafting economic, social, and cultural policies.

In 2019, WIPO noted that China had surpassed US as the source of the highest
patent applications filed with WIPO.[108] It was noted that the patent offices in China
received more than 46% of the global patent applications filed.[109] Further, mobile
manufacturing companies like Huawei, XTE, Vivo, Oppo, Xiaomi have their origin
in China.

5.2 Standard Setting in China

China has been seeking to set their own standards instead of relying on the international standards as this will shift the focus of impact on international trade and
corresponding legal framework from countries like US and EU to China.[110] These
domestic policies, court decisions related to SEPs and FRAND will have an impact

---

[108] WIPO, 'China Becomes Top Filer of International Patents in 2019 Amid Robust Growth for
WIPO's IP Services, Treaties and Finances' (WIPO 2020) PR/2020/848 <https://www.wipo.int/
pressroom/en/articles/2020/article_0005.html#:~:text=In%201999%2C%20WIPO%20received%
20276,Gurry%20noted> accessed 02 December 2020.

[109] WIPO, 'IP Facts and Figures' (WIPO, 2019) <https://www.wipo.int/edocs/pubdocs/en/
wipo_pub_943_2019.pdf> accessed 02 December 2020.

[110] Christopher S Gibson, 'Globalization and the Technology Standards Game: Balancing Concerns
of Protectionism and Intellectual Property in International Standards' (2007) NELLCO Legal
Scholarship Repository.

on the global market in the high-technology sector.[111] China has adopted two standards program with strategic goals including Chinese prominence in international technology market by 2050.[112] With the development of standards, Chinese companies are taking measures to protect and monetize their IPRs like the other developed nations. More IP cases are being filed in China than before.

The increase in cases has led the courts and policymakers to analyze the various disputes which are related to SEPs. One such dispute is the availability of injunctive relief in the hands of SEP holder. This weapon of injunction is the most powerful one in the SEP licensing process. The decision on the grant of injunction should be taken cautiously as this might go against the implementers forcing them to enter license which is less than the FRAND rates. If grant of injunction in infringement cases becomes too regressive toward the SEP holder, the implementer may indulge in reverse hold-up and be able to receive royalties which is less than FRAND rates.

To strike a balance between SEP holders and implementers, China needed to develop policies and guidelines. To achieve this objective Beijing People's High Court formulated guidelines that borrows principles discussed in cases like *Huawei v ZTE*. The decision that led to these guidelines is *IWNComm v Sony* which was the first case concerning the infringement of the SEP and injunction was granted to the SEP holder. Here, the court developed a fault-based approach, but the only drawback is that it is applicable to the cases only within the purview of Beijing's High People's Court of China. Further, in April 2018, the Guangdong High People's Court issued another set of guidelines which is one of the most comprehensive guidelines related to SEP disputes.

5.3 Framework for Injunctions

Patent litigation was previously based on the norm that permanent injunction will be granted if the infringement on the part of the implementers of a particular technology is proved. However, in a 2013 case *Huawei v IDC*, IDC has abused its dominant position during the licensing process. The court held that the IDC seeking injunction against Huawei was unlawful as Huawei was a willing licensee and acted in good faith during the licensing process. This decision left an impression that injunction cannot be granted in all cases and this power should be used judiciously. After this, the court started analyzing FRAND obligations in the SEP licensing practices.

Article 24(2) of the SPC Interpretation of Issues of Application of Laws in the handling of Patent Infringement Disputes (II) (SPC (II)) provides a FRAND-based

---

[111] Daniel Sokol and Wentong Zheng, '*FRAND (and Industrial Policy) in China*' in Jorge L. Contreras (ed), *Cambridge Handbook of Technical Standardization Law: Competition, Antitrust and Patents* (New York: Cambridge University Press 2017).

[112] Christopher S Gibson, '*Globalization and the Technology Standards Game: Balancing Concerns of Protectionism and Intellectual Property in International Standards*' (2007) NELLCO Legal Scholarship Repository.

defense to injunction proceedings. The judicial interpretation provides that an injunction is not to be granted during an ongoing negotiation process where (i) an SEP holder intentionally violates the FRAND obligations and (ii) the accused implementer is clearly not at fault. The judicial interpretation provides a way for the courts to assess the behavior of parties during negotiations prior to granting of injunctions in SEP-related disputes.[113]

The jurisprudence on SEP and FRAND-related issues in China is rapidly developing and courts continue to use their powers to shape up the antitrust framework. Another reason for China in developing the jurisprudence on these disputes is the pressure of complying with the foreign judgments. The decisions in the last few years resolve some of the disputes related to SEPs, but the issue arises when an SEP holder seeks injunction against the infringing implementer. There were several cases pending in the IP courts of China that implied that a lot had to be done for the development of FRAND jurisprudence in China.

The first case being *IWNComm* where fault-based approach was followed, and injunction was granted to the SEP holder against the infringement by an implementer. Sony was the licensee who wanted to license the standard held by IWNComm and therefore, entered negotiations but did not reach any agreement. Later, SEP holder filed an infringement suit against Sony in 2015.

The Beijing IP Court took note of the substantive negotiation process that the SEP holder carried out since 2009. The negotiation process continued from March 2009 to March 2015 where the SEP holder and implementer both exchanged e-mails regarding the negotiations. The parties on 7 April 2009 signed a confidential contract after which the SEP holder submitted a list of patents that the SEP holder believes to be infringed. The implementer on 14 July 2009 requested the SEP holder to provide a detailed information and a detailed list of claims to which the SEP holder promptly replied, but the implementer continued to ask for more detailed information.

The SEP holder on 6 June 2012 stated that two other parties had signed a confidential agreement on the same information in 2009. The implementer on 8 August 2012 informed the SEP holder that they did not find that they need to obtain a patent license and requested SEP holder to provide a claim comparison table. The parties continued negotiations till 23 December 2014 where the communication included issues of confidentiality agreement and patent licensing issues. The SEP holder also expressed their willingness to "consider providing a claim comparison table" based on signing a confidentiality agreement to which the implementer again responded by requesting the claim charts. The SEP holder requested for signing of confidentiality agreement first.

The Beijing IP Court put forth their views on the availability of injunctions to the SEP holder in the disputes related to SEPs. The court held that the implementer has been involved in the infringement of the SEP and indulged in the delaying tactics by prolonging the discussion on claim charts. The court suggested that the implementer has a rational basis to use the SEPs as a prospective licensee of a FRAND license but

---

[113] Li Zhongsheng, '*Patent Disputes and Article 24 of Judicial Interpretation II*' (*China Law Insight*, 21 April 2017).

such basis is grounded in good faith negotiations between the parties. The court ruled that if the parties have failed to reach an agreement and it is difficult to decide whether the implementer's use of SEP overrides the SEP holder's right to seek injunction, the court should look into the fault of both the parties during the negotiation process. To prevent the abuse of rights of injunction be an SEP holder, the court held that injunction would not be granted if both the parties are not at fault or if the SEP holder is at fault and not the implementer.

In a situation where both the parties are at fault then the court should calculate which party is more at fault. However, in this case a permanent injunction was granted to the SEP holder. After this decision, the Beijing High People's Court came up with guidelines which borrow the structure from *Huawei v ZTE*. These guidelines added more to the jurisprudence of SEP and FRAND licensing in China.

5.4 Beijing Guidelines, 2017

The Beijing Higher People's Court 'Guide to Patent Infringement Judgment' deals with judicial interpretations and guidelines related to injunctions in SEP disputes. The Guidelines under Articles 152–153 specifically provide the way injunctive relief will be applicable in situations where neither party has fault, or both parties are at fault during SEP licensing negotiations. The Guidelines are affirmative to the position of Beijing IP Court's approach in *IWNComm v Sony*.[114]

These guidelines include 153 articles that are divided into six aspects that cover a broad range of topics including determination of scope of protection and infringement of invention patents, utility model patents and design patents, determination of acts of patent infringement, and defense in patent infringement cases. The guidelines also deal with judicial interpretation and injunction in SEP disputes under the category of Non-infringement Defense (Articles 149–153). The guidelines affirm the decision in *IWNComm*.[115]

The SPC (II) issued in 2016 only dealt with FRAND commitments made under optional national or local standard and did not address the FRAND commitment for international standards made before an international SSO. Article 149 provides that the FRAND commitments made before an international SSO should be addressed in the same way as the national or local standards contemplated under Article 24 of the SPC (II).[116]

---

[114] Yin Li, Hui Zhang and James Yang, *'New Developments on SEP-Related Disputes in China'* (*Kluwer patent Blog*, 3 July 2017) <http://patentblog.kluweriplaw.com/2017/07/03/new-developments-sep-related-disputes-china/; http://www.patentexp.com/?p=799> accessed 02 December 2020.

[115] Yin Li, Hui Zhang & James Yang, *'New Developments on SEP Related Disputes in China'* (*Kluwer Patent Blog*, 3 July 2017) <http://patentblog.kluweriplaw.com/2017/07/03/new-developments-sep-related-disputes-china/?print=pdf> accessed 02 December 2020.

[116] SPC Interpretation of Issues of Application of Laws in the Handling of Patent Infringement Disputes (II) (SPC (II)), art 24 <http://www.glo.com.cn/en/content/details_13_673.html> accessed 02 December 2020.

Further, Article 150 provides that it is not only the SEP holder who needs to follow FRAND commitment but also the implementer also has the responsibility to negotiate on good faith and conclude a licensing agreement. The concept of good faith emerges from Article 7 of the General Principles of Civil Law in China[117] and is an advisory norm and may help in judging the faults of parties in the process of negotiation. While adjudging fault in an ongoing litigation, the court shall take into consideration whether both parties negotiated in good faith.

The guidelines under Articles 152–153 specifically provide the way injunctive relief will be allowed in situations where neither party is at fault, or both parties are at fault during the negotiation process of licensing SEPs. According to the guidelines, there are certain circumstances under which an SEP holder may violate its FRAND licensing commitments. While deciding on the injunction application of the SEP holder, these guidelines sought to provide a fault-based approach to the courts to determine the party at fault. The conditions are very similar to those established by the CJEU in *Huawei*.[118]

The Guidelines provide the specific circumstances under which it may be determined that the SEP holder has violated its FRAND licensing obligations. The first condition was that if the implementer was not informed in writing about the infringing patent and the scope of such infringement (Notice Stage).[119] This is similar to the requirement of notice under *Huawei* where an SEP holder is required to send a notice containing details of the infringing activity of the implementer.[120] Secondly, the SEP holder will be at fault if he has not provided specific conditions under which the implementer can be permitted to use the patent after implementer has expressed his willingness to accept the negotiated patent license (Offer Stage). The guidelines also provide that the SEP holder should respond to the implementers response in due time corresponding to the business practices and trading habits. The Guidelines suggest that during the license process if the SEP holder hinders or interrupt the process without any reasonable reason, he shall be at fault.[121]

As the Guidelines took note of the Beijing Court's ruling in IWNComm, they also provided a scenario where the implementer is also at fault during the negotiation along with the SEP holder. In such situation, the judge shall determine the degree of fault of both the parties. The implementer shall be at fault in the negotiation process if upon receipt of the written license conditions the implementer did not reply within a reasonable time (Response Stage).[122] The response can be acceptance of the proposed offer, or the implementer shall propose new licensing conditions (Counteroffer). The implementer will be at fault in negotiation process if it blocks delays or refuses to participate in negotiation process without any reasonable ground or claim any clearly unreasonable condition resulting in inability to reach a conclusion during the

---

[117] SPC (II), art 7 <http://www.npc.gov.cn/englishnpc/Law/2007-12/12/content_1383941.htm>.

[118] *Huawei.*

[119] Guidelines (n), art 151.

[120] *Huawei* (n), para 61.

[121] Guidelines (n), art 152.

[122] Ibid.

licensing process. Further the Guidelines provided that in case neither party has fault, the implementer will deposit an amount of its proposed royalty in the court to avoid injunction.[123]

The Guidelines provided by the Beijing Court are like the Court of Justice of the European Union (CJEU) guidelines in *Huawei* about framework of licensing negotiations. In addition, the ambiguities are of similar nature, for example, the Beijing Court's guideline also do not provide about the nature or content of the offer that is to be made by the SEP holder to implementer. *IWNComm* has already established that claim charts need not be included in the infringement notice if it can be assumed that implementer will be able to self-evaluate the patents with the materials in hand. The Guidelines provide that there should not be any hindrance on unreasonable ground, but the discretion of determining those grounds has not been made clear and may require further clarification. The qualification of not providing any unreasonable condition leading to the termination of negotiation process is also subjective.

Interim payments are usually made by the implementer to secure the interest of SEP holder. However, the guidelines leave it up to the implementer to determine the amount of payment to be made[124] which could be problematic in situations where the implementer has also challenged the validity of the SEP in dispute. In China, an implementer can bring an invalidation proceeding before the Patent Re-examination Board. It is a common practice in several jurisdictions for an implementer to challenge the validity of the patent during SEP dispute, which would create problem for the determination of the interim payment.[125]

The Chinese court would require both parties to propose reasonable conditions during negotiations without suggesting further guidelines explaining 'reasonable conditions'. In another case of *Huawei v Samsung*[126] the court granted injunction to the SEP holder. The case concerns two 4G-related SEPs owned by Huawei. The negotiation process continued for six years to enter a cross licensing deal. Although a translated English copy of the judgment is still not available, a detailed summary of the judgment has been posted in several blogs and Chinese law firms.

The court in *Huawei v Samsung*[127] found the implementer to be engaged in delaying tactics by delaying the procedures with the insistence on bundling both SEPs and non-SEPs together. The implementer was also said to delay the technical discussion by not responding in a timely manner to the claim charts provided by the SEP holder.[128] The implementer also delayed submitting the license offer and

---

[123] Guidelines (n 18), art 153.

[124] Guidelines (n 18), art 152.

[125] There have been cases in India and Germany where the Implementers have challenged the validity of patents during infringement proceedings. In *IWNComm*, Sony failed to challenge the validity of patent on jurisdictional issues.

[126] *Huawei v Samsung*.

[127] Ibid.

[128] Jacob Schindler, '*Full Judgment in Huawei v Samsung Details Why Shenzhen court Hit Korean Company with SEP Injunction*' (*iam*, 3 April 2017) <http://www.iam-media.com/blog/Detail.aspx?g=31514eba-a4cf-4861-b0c2-1210e49ccb7c> accessed 02 December 2020.

counteroffer and also rejected the SEP holder's offer to submit the dispute to binding arbitration three times.[129] The approach of Shenzhen Court, while determining that the implementer was at fault during the negotiation, was very close to the framework provided in Huawei and the Beijing high Court's guideline on an SEP infringement case.

5.5   *Guangdong Guidelines, 2018*

The Guangdong Higher People's Court issued "Guidelines on Trials of Standard Patent Dispute Cases" in 2018. The Guangdong Guidelines required courts in Guangzhou, Shenzhen, and Guangdong to apply the fault-based liability framework to resolve disputes related to the FRAND royalties.[130] The most important feature of these guidelines is that it includes the principles laid down in decisions in countries such as US, UK, CJEU and China.[131] Apart from the issues related to injunction and fault-based framework, it also addresses issues related to the determination of FRAND royalty and antitrust issues related to the conduct of SEP holder.

The Guangdong guidelines lay down clear norms in relation to the injunctive relief. It will monitor the behavior of both the parties during the negotiation process to find out whether it is the fault of the SEP holder or implementer. The entire negotiation process is taken into consideration, the time taken in the negotiation of the license, communication between the parties, and reasons for failure in reaching an agreement.[132] It affirms the principles laid down in *Huawei v ZTE* and *Unwired Planet v Huawei*. It requires the parties to negotiate in good faith. In all the SEP disputes, Guangdong High People's Court will take note of the contribution of the SEP holder and protect his/her rights, but it will balance the interests of SEP holder, implementer, and the public.

The Guidelines requires courts to take into consideration the following factors to determine the FRAND rate—"comparable licensing agreements; 'market value' of the relevant SEPs in dispute; and licensing conditions of comparable patent pools".[133]

It has a similar approach to Beijing guidelines when the fault is of the implementer. The guidelines indicate that there is a need to negotiate licenses without getting involved in the delaying tactics as this could frustrate the SEP holder's efforts to enter into an agreement of license with the implementer. Another fault of the implementer is when it refuses to sign an NDA without any reason and proposes an unreasonable

---

[129] Ibid.

[130] King Mallesons & Wood, '*Guangdong High People's Court Issued a Guideline for Trial of Sep Disputes | China Law Insight*' (updated 2018-05-23).

[131] Ibid., *Huawei v ZTE, Unwired Planet, Motorola v Microsoft, TCL v Ericsson, IWNComm, Huawei v Samsung*.

[132] Article 11, Guangdong Guidelines.

[133] Ibid.

licensing condition.[134] An NDA is one of the important elements of a license, and refusal to enter one indicates that implementer does not want to conclude the licensing agreement. The determination of fault of the SEP holder is like what is laid down in the Beijing Guidelines.

There are instances when it is either difficult to find the fault of either party or when the fault is of both the parties. In such situations, the court compares the degree of fault of both the parties, the impact of the fault on the negotiation process, the relation between the fault and the breakdown of the negotiation.[135]

The Guidelines also allows the courts to set worldwide royalty rates if the parties to the dispute agree to it. In addition, the court could ask the SEP holder to provide evidence related to the determination of the royalty rates. In case the SEP holder fails to provide evidence related to the calculation of the royalty rate, then the court can determine the same relying on the evidence provided by the implementer.

According to the Guidelines, if both the parties are unable to decide a reasonable royalty rate, then either of the parties can apply to the court for the determination of a FRAND encumbered royalty rate. If such an issue arises, Guangdong High People's Court will fix a global royalty rate, provided that the other party does not raise any objections to it.[136] The Guidelines did not elaborate on reasonable oppositions to a Chinese court, therefore, they determine the royalty rates beyond its jurisdictions. This means that implementers would approach domestic courts to determine reasonable royalty rates which as a result becomes inconvenient for the SEP holders of those countries especially those which do not believe in the Chinese courts.

Further, objections filed by the SEP holders that inconvenience is caused to them by the determination of the royalty rate by Chinses courts does not fulfill the reasonable criteria. However, the Guangdong courts in such situations have adopted the approach on *Unwired Planet* and *TCL v Ericsson*. Therefore, the SEP holders who claim such an inconvenience should include a clause that such disputes should be resolved through arbitration.[137]

Guangdong guidelines also states that royalties should be set based on multiple factors. Royalty can be determined based on the assessment of comparable licenses. While examining the comparable license courts are required to take into consideration "factors such as, entities involved in the licensing transactions, relevance between the transacting subjects and genuine interests of the parties negotiating license agreement".[138]

The guidelines requires the courts to consider:

the differences in terms of licensing background, licensing content and the terms involved in the licensing agreements. To determine the market value of the SEPs involved in the

---

[134] Article 14(2), Guangdong Guidelines.

[135] Article 12(4), Guangdong Guidelines.

[136] Article 16, Guangdong Guidelines.

[137] Ben Ni & Wood Mallesons, '*The Guangdong High Peoples Court Guideline for Sep Disputes: A Primer*', Managing Intellectual Property (2018).

[138] Article 20, Guangdong Guidelines.

transaction the court is required to take into consideration the ratio of the SEPs involved in the licensing process to all the SEPs involved in the standard and the total royalty rates of all the SEPs This information regarding the ratio has to be provided by either the SEP holder or implementer. For the determination of the total royalty rates, the court needs to consider the cumulative royalty relevant to the participants involved in the development of the standard.[139]

The Guangdong guidance allows courts to stay proceedings when the parties to a dispute agree to continue their negotiations on the royalty rates. The court may resume the proceedings if one party feels that the negotiations cannot go any further. If either of the party is of the opinion that the opposing party has key evidence to determine royalty rates, then that party could request court to order the opposing party to reveal such evidence. If the opposing party refuses to reveal evidence without any reasonable cause, then the court would determine the royalty rate based on the evidence provided by the party that has requested the intervention of the court.[140] This approach by the Guangdong court suggests that it favors a consensual approach before they move to determine the royalty rates on their own.

For the determination of an anticompetitive effect, the Guangdong Guidelines requires the antitrust agencies to consider Anti-Monopoly Law of the People's Republic of China. The Guidelines further provide that the courts should examine the anticompetitive effect of conduct of parties on a case-by-case basis.[141] Seeking injunctive relief itself does not amount to abuse of dominant position by an SEP holder. The conduct of the negotiating parties is taken into consideration while deciding on the abuse of dominant position. It is also important to consider whether SEP holder is putting pressure on the implementer to agree to the unfair licensing terms or exorbitant royalty rates which is above the FRAND royalty rate and hence, all these instances leading to the restriction of competition in the market.[142]

Although Beijing Guidelines and Guangdong Guidelines have a similar approach regarding the fault-based approach toward resolving SEP disputes, the Guangdong guidelines have elaborated on some issues which were not being addresses in the Beijing guidelines. These issues include the determination of FRAND royalty and determination of abuse of dominant position. It also develops on the fault-based approach taken up by Beijing guidelines. The drawback of Beijing guidelines was that it only applied to the Beijing High People's Court but same is with the Guangdong guidelines which also apply only to Guangdong and Shenzhen region, but some of the leading telecommunications companies are headquartered in these regions. The Guangdong guidelines also stated that Chinese courts are so keen in solving the SEP disputes as they could decide the global royalty rate. It also aims in balancing the interests of the SEP holders and implementers.

---

[139] Article 23, Guangdong Guidelines.

[140] Article 19, Guangdong Guidelines.

[141] Adrian Emch, 'New SEP Guidelines from Guangdong' (Kluwer Competition Law Blog, 1 June 2018) <http://competitionlawblog.kluwercompetitionlaw.com/2018/06/01/new-sep-guidelines-guangdong/> accessed 02 December 2020.

[142] Article 29, Guangdong Guidelines.

5.6 The Chinese Antimonopoly Law and SEPs

On 29th December 2018, China's State Administration for Market Regulation (SAMR) had announced 16 typical cases regarding the abuse of administrative power to exclude and restrict competition in 2018. In 2019, the SAMR has drafted a slew of provisions in its bid to boost the Anti-Monopoly Law enforcement and to prevent and restrain monopolistic agreements in the country. On 3rd January 2019, the SAMR published the draft of "Provisions on Prohibition of Monopolistic Agreements" for public comments. Also on 3rd January, the SAMR issued the "Notice on Antitrust Enforcement Authorization", granting general authorization to provincial-level market regulators.

On 18th January 2019, the SAMR put on the public domain the draft "Provisions on Prohibition of Abusing Administrative Power to Eliminate and Restrict Competition" for comments. On 30th January 2019, the SAMR publicized the "Provisions on Prohibition of Abuse of Market Dominant Position" for public comments. SAMR promoted on 26th June 2019 and published the "Interim Rules on Prohibition against Monopoly Agreements (the MLA Rules)" and the "Interim Rules on Prohibition against Abuse of Dominant Market Position (the DMP Rules)" on 1 July 2019.

More recently, in August 2020, the Anti-Monopoly Bureau under SAMR released Anti-Monopoly Guidelines. The Anti-Monopoly Guidelines on Intellectual Property Rights ("IPR Guidelines") was released with the objective of "seeking much needed clarity on several contentious issues at the crossroads of competition law and IP law". The IPR Guidelines cover five topics, namely "general rules, Intellectual property ("IP") related agreements which may eliminate or restrict competition, IP-related abuses by owners holding a dominant market position, IP-related merger filings and other situations involving IP-related issue".[143]

The SAMR will have to assess the market dominance of patent owners. The following factors will have to be taken into account to assess market dominance: "the market value and the scope and depth of application of the relevant standard; the level of compatibility of the relevant standard; existence of substitutable standards or technologies, and the accessibility and switching costs thereof; the nature of dependence on certain industry standards, and the possibility of replacing the SEPs for the relevant standard".[144]

An anticompetitive effect, according to these guidelines, is likely to be found when the owner of an essential patent seeking injunctive relief (with dominant position in the relevant market) against potential standard implementers for not fulfilling demand

---

[143] Cheng Liu, et al., 'China's IP Antitrust Guidelines Released to the Public' (China Law Insight August 2020) <https://www.chinalawinsight.com/2020/08/articles/antitrust/chinas-ip-antitrust-guidelines-released-to-the-public/> accessed 02 December 2020.
[144] Ibid.

of paying royalties that are unfairly high. To assess competition effects of injunction applications, the SAMR would consider the following factors[145]:

- How the parties behaved during the negotiation, and their true intention reflected by their behavior;
- Commitments attached to the relevant SEPs (e.g., the FRAND commitments);
- Terms of licensing proposed by the parties during negotiation;
- The impact of the motion for injunction on the licensing negotiation; and
- The impact of the motion for injunction on competition in the downstream market and the interest of consumers.

In practice, courts in China carefully scrutinize the entire process of negotiation along with the licensing conditions presented by the parties to make a decision on whether the patent owner is fulfilling the FRAND promise or not.[146]

6 Japan

6.1 A Brief Overview of Japan's Patent System

Japan has adopted the continental legal framework with three written codes—the Patent Law, which talks about the rights of the patent holders; the Anti-Monopoly Act to regulate the general principles against monopoly and unfair trades; and the Designation of Unfair Trade Practices (Designation), which includes detailed principles on unfair trades and various guidelines specifying the criteria for implementing Anti-Monopoly Act and the Designation.

The patent law does not talk about technological standard and there are only few provisions which deal with SEPs under Articles 92 and 93 which talks about compulsory licensing for the improvement of inventions and public interest, respectively. Article 93 does not work on any specific rules, but the lawyers and policymakers follow a report published under Foreign Capital Council in 1968 which states "that such license should be permitted only when it is directly connected to the lives of the citizens and the refusal of the license would result in crippling the development of the related industries."[147] Article 92 got suspended as a result of the US-Japan

---

[145] Jones Day, '*China Publishes Anti-Monopoly Guidelines on Intellectual Property*' <https://www.jonesday.com/-/media/files/publications/2020/10/china-publishes-antimonopoly-guidelines-on-int ellectual-property/files/china-publishes-antimonopoly-guidelines-on-ip/fileattachment/china-pub lishes-antimonopoly-guidelines-on-ip.pdf> accessed 02 December 2020.

[146] Jones Day, '*China Publishes Anti-Monopoly Guidelines on Intellectual Property*' <https://www.jonesday.com/-/media/files/publications/2020/10/china-publishes-antimonopoly-guidelines-on-int ellectual-property/files/china-publishes-antimonopoly-guidelines-on-ip/fileattachment/china-pub lishes-antimonopoly-guidelines-on-ip.pdf> accessed 02 December 2020.

[147] Ashish Bharadwaj & Tohru Yoshioka-Kobayashi, 'Regulating Standard Essential Patents in Implementer-Oriented Countries: Insights from Japan and India' in Ashish Bharadwaj, Vishwas

Agreement in 1994. It is because of these restrictions; no compulsory license has been directed so far.

Some portion of the SEP issues has been regulated by the Anti-Monopoly Act. In 2007, the Japan Fair Trade Commission (JFTC) released guidelines titled "Guidelines for the Use of Intellectual Property under the Anti-Monopoly Act". Despite being relevant and ahead of time in the global IP landscape, there were almost no substantive discussions on these guidelines until 2016.

6.2 Guidelines for the Use of Intellectual Property Under the Japanese Antimonopoly Act

The first significant policy change on SEPs in technologically agile Japan was introduced in 2015. It dawned on the Japan Fair Trade Commission (JFTC) that setting ground rules and providing clarity on the regulation of SEPs was paramount, and a draft of partial amendment of "Guidelines for the Use of Intellectual Property under the Antimonopoly Act" was released. It also sought views from a variety of national and international stakeholders, including the civil society, government departments, industry associations/societies working on IP, legal scholars and practitioners. Many Japanese companies—prolific innovators/standard contributors and early adopters/standard implementers—have close backward and forward linkages with tech and non-tech companies around the world, all of whom took a careful note of the guidelines and its potential impact. One swift and welcome result was that the JFTC modified its stance based on some of the reactions to publish a revised draft of the amendments in January 2016. The revision sufficiently clarified that seeking injunctive relief against licensees that were willing to get on board, and, in general, refusing to offer a license for patents essential to a standard would amount to unfair trade practices.

6.3 Recent Technical Studies on IP and SEPs in Japan

In 2015, an IP advisory board under the leadership of the then Prime Minister of Japan, initiated a series of discussions under an Intellectual Property Dispute Resolution System Review Committee with emphasis on some of the major IP issues in a dispute including procedural aspects of the investigation, quantitative assessment of damages, and restrictions on injunctive relief. In the Committee's final report released in March 2016, a unified mechanism of restrictions on IP rights was not supported, and no legal changes were recommended. The report was rather unambiguous in its observation that any unified framework of restrictions may adversely affect the

H. Devaiah and Indranath Gupta (eds.), *Multi-Dimensional Approaches Towards New Technology* (Springer 2019).

incentives for innovation resulting in second-order impact on standard setting and development.

Attention was given to understand the rapidly growing 'Internet of Things' (IoT) model of technological advancement globally and the 'Fourth Industrial Revolution' (4IR) in Japan where digital interconnectivity among industries, devices, and services may bring up issues concerning SEPs sooner than later. The experts felt that there is an urgent need to address SEP licensing issues that are now going beyond the wireless industry to involve other economy heavyweights including industries in the automobiles, electronic appliances, and industrial equipment.

Keeping this in mind, in 2016, the Japanese Ministry of Economy, Trade and Industry (METI) set up a working group on the IP system to study several issues of contemporary relevance such as data protection laws and regulations, protection of IP underlying innovation in artificial intelligence-enabled technologies, and creative resolutions to disputes in licensing of SEPs. In the following year, the working group published its report that specifically addressed some very important concerns around standard essential patents in Japan. This included the rising number of SEPs, limited scope of SEP pools that has implications on licensing negotiations, impact of these developments on the small and medium enterprises of Japan, the cost to society from these patent disputes, and the role of non-practicing patent entities in disrupting the licensing of SEPs in Japan.

Parallel to this study of the working group, a report from the IP Dispute Resolution Committee found a fair amount of skepticism regarding a uniform framework of restrictions on SEPs. In a surprising turn of events that caught many who were engaged with the topic globally, the Committee proposed a new and different system of resolution of disputes on SEPs. In this special ADR (alternate dispute resolution) system, the Japanese government would effectively determine the rate of royalties that were fair and reasonable. Their report stated that:

> It will be necessary to take initiatives to deal with SEPs, which will become a part of public infrastructure in line with the popularization of IoT. We will need to find ways to reduce the costs of licensing negotiations and settling disputes that may hinder the smooth use of the SEPs. First, the government will consider introducing an ADR system (licensing award system for SEPs) designed to deal with disputes on licensing of SEPs, which have a significant influence on society. Under this system, government will work on disputes between patent holders and possible licensees based on request by the latter, when the parties cannot reach agreements on licensing, deciding appropriate licensing fees of SEPs with due care of not unfairly harm the interests of the patent holders.[148]

With IoT becoming all pervasive, there was a need to evolve a framework that would enable the industry to develop standards more smoothly so that it can facilitate the development of the social infrastructure. A special ADR system was proposed[149] "for determining reasonable license fees for SEPs with significant social impact,

---

[148] Ministry of Economy, Trade and Industry, '*Intellectual Property System in Consideration of the Fourth Industrial Revolution*' (April 2017) 21 <http://www.meti.go.jp/press/2017/04/201704 19002/20170419002.html> accessed 02 December 2020.

[149] Although the document is silent about the governing body of the ADR, a Japanese newspaper leaked out that the JPO will establish a new 'adjudication' system. '*License ryo kuni ga saitei :*

while paying attention not to give undue impact on the right of patentees, with a view to submitting a bill to the National Diet (the Japanese house of representatives)".[150] The JPO clarified that the two ADR systems would be used, wherein one would be used to resolve the FRAND royalties dispute and the other system would be used to resolve other general disputes.[151]

This too followed heated debates. While some members from the industry and industry association supported the idea of 'SEP adjudication',[152] some industrial associations raised objection citing concerns regarding effectiveness, coverage, complexity, expertise, and the overall impact on the society.[153] The critics explained that first, the new adjudication system would cover only Japanese patents most of which, particularly in the high-tech industries, tend to have expansive international patent families; second, the complexity of the protracted legal process if dispute resolution would not costly in time and resources; third, the JPO suffered from lack of expertise in adjudicating matters pertaining to determining FRAND royalties and damages; and finally, constitution of a public ADR forum for matters that ought to be managed privately will affect businesses. The Japan Business Federation ("Keidanren") went one step further in its warning that the proposed SEP adjudication process will be perceived as a process of compulsory licensing thereby distorting incentives to innovate and creating a negative perception of innovation and IP ecosystem of Japan in the international community.

In the face of intense objections, a complementary approach was sought by the JPO that promised to not keep the guideline legally binding.[154] Later that year, in November 2017, recognizing the inherent unfairness of the system for SEP holders and the difficulties in accurately determining FRAND royalties, the idea of introducing the SEP adjudication system was kept in abeyance.[155]

Finally, the JPO suggested introducing guidelines for facilitating negotiations for licensing of SEPs and constituting an advisory system to determine essentiality of

---

hyouzyun kikaku ni saiyou no tokkyo [The government arbitrage the royalty rate of SEPs]' Nikkei Newspaper (27 April 2017) (In Japanese).

[150] Ibid. 28–29.

[151] Japan Patent Office, '*Shorthand Notes of the 20th meeting of Patent System Subcommittee of Industrial Structure Council*' <https://www.jpo.go.jp/shiryou/toushin/shingikai/pdf/tokkyo_seido_menu/newtokkyo_020.pdf> accessed 02 December 2020.

[152] In the debate in Intellectual Property Strategy Headquarters, one advisory who are from chemical industry sector and corporate executive association was in the favor of the introduction of ADR.

[153] See comments from Japan Electronics and Information Technology Industries Association (JEITA) <https://www.jpo.go.jp/shiryou/toushin/shingikai/pdf/newtokkyo_shiry-ou22/01.pdf> and Keidanren <https://www.jpo.go.jp/shiryou/toushin/shingikai/pdf/new-tokkyo_shiryou22/02.pdf> (In Japanese).

[154] NTT Data Institute of Management Consulting, Inc., '*Kuni no gyousei kikan ga kouhyou shita guideline tou no zittai haaku no tameno chosa* [A survey report on guidelines published by the government]' <http://www.soumu.go.jp/main_content/000424429.pdf> accessed 02 December 2020 (In Japanese).

[155] '*Tokkyocho ga ADR seido miokuri: License ryo no settei konnan*n (JPO gave up the introduction of ADR because of the difficulty in setting reasonable royalty)' *Nikkan Kogyo Shinbun* (27 November 2017) (In Japanese).

the patent claimed to be essential to a standard.[156] While clarifying that no new regulations were being put in place, efforts will be made to understand how these matters are being adjudicated in courts around the world to improve the understanding of the behavior and actions of prospective licensors and licensees. This process culminated in the 'Guide to Licensing Negotiations involving Standard Essential Patents' in March 2018.[157] We have written previously that the final version that was published within four months was "a reflection of the JPO's attitude to be an objective information provider to support SMEs or large firms outside the telecommunication industry".[158]

6.4   Guide to Licensing Negotiations Involving SEPs

The draft Guide to Licensing Negotiations involving SEPs of the Japanese Patent Office[159] offered insights and instructions on issues that were at the core of the SEP litigations during the period of 2015–2018. The 2018 Guidelines were futuristic in their vision and drew attention toward a variety of methodologies that could be used to value patents in a digitally connected, automated IoT-enabled world. The drafters had the foresight to understand the reliance on technical interoperable standards by companies and organizations beyond the conventional ICT industry, and to contemplate the contentious issues that may emerge among these stakeholders. For Japan the challenges were more intense. While, historically, the innovative Japanese firms were the patent holders and standard contributors for large parts of the emerging world (including China and India), they were gradually becoming patent licensees and standard implementers for the tech-intensive European and American (even Chinese) firms in the twenty-first century. The implication of this dilemma in policymaking was that Japan had to carefully strike a balance between the rights of SEP holders and SEP implementers, while preserving the incentives to innovate. More specifically, the policymakers, regulators, and even the courts in Japan faced difficult questions. Do royalty rates and base should vary depending on the end-use of the technology? Are the resulting royalties FRAND complaint? What is the most robust technique to ensure and ascertain this compliance? Should the contributions of patents vary in a standard, will (and how) the royalties change? The JPO

---

[156] Japan Patent Office, 'Hyozyun hissu tokkyo wo meguru kadai to seidoteki taiou ni tsuite [Policy actions on SEP related issues]' <https://www.jpo.go.jp/shiryou/toushin/shingikai/pdf/newtokkyo_shiryou23/01.pdf> accessed 02 December 2020 (In Japanese).

[157] Japan Patent Office, 'Draft of Guide to Licensing Negotiations Involving Standard Es sential Patents' (2018) <https://www.jpo.go.jp/iken/pdf/180308_hyoujun/sep_guide_draft_en.pdf> accessed 02 December 2020.

[158] Ibid.

[159] Japan Patent Office, 'Guide to Licensing Negotiations Involving Standard Essential Patents' (2018) <http://www.jpo.go.jp/iken/pdf/180308_hyoujun/sep_guide_draft_en.pdf> accessed 02 December 2020.

embraced the view that future technologies and their spectacularly diverse use necessitate charging different royalties without being discriminatory. The draft Guidelines state that "it is not discriminatory for a patent holder to apply different royalties for products that enjoy the capacity of the technology either wholly (e.g. self-driving car, remote surgery) or partially (e.g. smart meter) even if they use the same standard technology".[160]

The Guide to Licensing Negotiations involving Standard Essential Patents came into effect from 5th June 2018. The JPO noted:

> The Guide aims to enhance transparency and predictability, facilitate negotiations between rights holders and implementers, and help prevent or quickly resolve disputes concerning the licensing of standard essential patents (SEPs) which are essential in implementing standards in the field of wireless communications and the like.[161]

6.5 Guidelines on the 'Fair Value Calculation of SEP for Multi-component Products'

The "Fair Value Calculation of SEP for Multi-Component Products" Guidelines aims to facilitate the negotiation of FRAND licenses by providing a guidance on how to calculate SEP royalties for multi-component products.[162] The guidelines relies on three principles to calculate the fair value—"first, the parties to a licensing agreement should be decided based on the concept of "license to all". Second, the royalty should be calculated using a "top-down" approach. Third, the royalty should be calculated based on the portion to which the SEP technology contributes (contribution rate) in the value of the main product that implements the SEP technology".[163]

---

[160] Japan Patent Office, 'Announcement for release of "Guide to Licensing Negotiations involving Standard Essential Patents"' (5 June 2018) <https://www.jpo.go.jp/e/system/laws/rule/guideline/patent/seps-tebiki.html> accessed 02 December 2020.

[161] Japan Patent Office, 'Announcement for Release of "Guide to Licensing Negotiations involving Standard Essential Patents "' (5 June 2018) <https://www.jpo.go.jp/e/system/laws/rule/guideline/patent/seps-tebiki.html> accessed 02 December 2020.

[162] Enrico Bonadio & Luke McDonagh, Japan: Guidelines on the 'Fair Value Calculation of SEP for Multi-Component Products' <http://patentblog.kluweriplaw.com/2020/06/15/japan-guidelines-on-the-fair-value-calculation-of-sep-for-multi-component-products/> accessed 02 December 2020.

[163] Ministry of Economy, Trade and Industry, 'Guide to Fair Value Calculation of Standard Essential Patents for Multi-Component Products' <https://www.meti.go.jp/policy/mono_info_service/mono/smart_mono/sep/200421sep_fairvalue_hp_eng.pdf> accessed 02 December 2020.

Chapter 2
SSOs' Role in Facilitating IP Policy Measures

1 Introduction

Generally speaking, standards are adopted to reduce transaction costs for several implementers and increase interoperability among devices and platforms. Standards make our lives as consumers easier. For instance, a Wi-Fi-enabled smartphone device will connect to a Wi-Fi connection regardless of the jurisdiction. It has happened because Wi-Fi is a standard, which has been unanimously adopted by all stakeholders. There are technical standards adopted through several standard setting organizations, and there are standards adopted through market demand, which have evolved with time. Standard setting organizations (SSOs) play a crucial role in operationalizing a standard. The stages through which a standard is operationalized are often fraught with uncertainty, and a lot depends on the internal structure of an SSO. The most significant contributor to the entire process is the IPR policies adopted by each of these SSOs. This chapter provides a glimpse of these IPR policies of SSOs in three different jurisdictions, i.e., Europe, the United States, and India. These policies show their diverse nature and often lead to complex end-results.

2 Why Do We Need a Standard?

While there could be different ways of explaining the meaning assigned to 'standard,'[1] there is no doubt that interoperability is the key to any standard's success.

---

[1] According to Mark Lemley, "… standard rather broadly as any set of technical specifications that either provides or in intended to provide a common design for a product or process", Mark A. Lemley, 'Intellectual Property Rights and Standard-Setting Organizations' (2002) 90 California Law Review 1889, 1896.

© The Author(s) 2022
V. H. Bharadwaj et al., *Locating Legal Certainty in Patent Licensing*,
https://doi.org/10.1007/978-981-15-0181-4_2

The OECD's standard definition points that "… interoperability standards designed to ensure that two or more related products or processes may fit and operate with each other."[2]

In the context of ICT, which is also the focus of this chapter and the book, the definition provided by the European Telecommunications Standards Institute (ETSI) report is apt. It suggests that "a standard defines requirements, specifications, guidelines or characteristics for a determined material, product, process or service."[3] Further, they went on to identify the above requirements for the role of a standard setting body. The report suggests that "[formal] standards are developed by SDOs, which involve selected stakeholders in the item to be standardized, such as manufacturers, providers, consumers, and regulators, with possible contributions from academics and professional users."[4] According to this definition, the working of a standard setting body should have a deliberative structure. According to the report, such an adopted structure would ensure a fair and transparent process, aiming to build a certain consensus among various stakeholders.[5]

Standards are mainly laid down by using de jure (formal) and de facto mechanisms.[6] De facto standards are established through a process of choice exercised by consumers. It involves a competitive process where consumers decide their preference over existing standards.[7] This standard-making process generally develops through uncoordinated efforts contrary to a consensual standard adopted by various stakeholders in the case of de jure or a formal standard. De facto standard results from a unilateral adoption of a technology by a market for multiple reasons.[8] It may

---

[2] OECD Policy Roundtables, 'Standard Setting' 2010 DAF/COMP (2010) 33, 9 <www.oecd.org/daf/competition/47381304.pdf> accessed 1 January 2021.

[3] Dr habil Nizar Abdelkaf and others, *Understanding ICT Standardization: Principles and Practice* (ETSI 2018) 12 <www.etsi.org/images/files/Education/Understanding_ICT_Standardization_LoResWeb_20190524.pdf> accessed 1 January 2021.

[4] Ibid.

[5] Ibid.

[6] Ibid.; Valerio Torti, *Intellectual Property Rights and Competition in Standard Setting: Objectives and Tensions* (Routledge 2018) 50.

[7] Donald E Knebel, 'Standard Setting Organizations and Competition Laws: Lessons and Suggestions from the United States' in Ashish Bharadwaj, Vishwas H. Devaiah and Indranath Gupta (eds.), *Complications and Quandaries in the ICT Sector: Standard Essential Patents and Competition Issues* (Springer International 2018) 141.

[8] US Department of Justice and Federal Trade Commission, 'Antitrust Enforcement and Intellectual Property Rights: Promoting Innovation and Competition' (2017) 34 <www.ftc.gov/sites/default/files/documents/reports/antitrust-enforcement-and-intellectual-property-rights-promoting-innovation-and-competition-report.s.department-justice-and-federal-trade-commission/p040101promotinginnovationandcompetitionrpt0704.pdf> accessed 1 January 2021; Carl Shapiro and Hal R Varian, 'The Art of Standards War' (1999) 41 California Management Review 8.

result in a unilateral adoption of technology by the market,[9] leading to a de facto monopoly.[10]

De jure standard setting process can happen either through government intervention or through a consensual standard setting mandate undertaken by a standard setting body.[11] Standard developed at a standard setting body evolves through a set procedure of rules to instill fairness in the entire process.[12]

The option of interoperability between different devices is materialized through the adoption of standards. As a result of standards, companies are incentivized to manufacture products that are compatible with each other. The manufacturing cost is reduced considerably due to the lessened cost of acquiring technical information and enabling efficient product design.[13] Therefore, standards would help producers improve the innovation ecosystem by promoting the interoperability of products, services, and processes.[14] Standards help reduce product development time, develop the quality of a product, and help producers trade in open crossborder markets.[15] Companies producing products based on standards allow them to work efficiently, leading to greater consumer satisfaction.[16] The interoperability achieved through the adoption of a standard product protects consumers and helps increase positive network effects.[17] It means standards would entail that a product is widely used, thereby raising demands and usefulness among its users.[18]

---

[9] OECD Policy Roundtables, 'Standard Setting' 2010 DAF/COMP (2010) 33, 20 <www.oecd.org/daf/competition/47381304.pdf> accessed 1 January 2021.

[10] Daniel J Gifford, 'Developing Models for a Coherent Treatment of Standard-Setting Issues Under the Patent, Copyright, and Antitrust Laws' (2003) 43 IDEA 331, 338.

[11] Ibid.; OECD Policy Roundtables, OECD Policy Roundtables, 'Standard Setting' 2010 DAF/COMP (2010) 33, 23 <www.oecd.org/daf/competition/47381304.pdf> accessed 1 January 2021; Justus Baron and Daniel Spulber, 'Technology Standards and Standards Organizations: Introduction to the Searle Centre Database' (2015) 3 Northwestern Law & Economic Research Paper No. 17-16, 5 <http://www.law.northwestern.edu/research-faculty/searlecenter/innovationeconomics/documents/Baron_Spulber_Searle%20Center_Database.pdf> accessed 1 January 2021.

[12] Daniel J Gifford, 'Developing Models for a Coherent Treatment of Standard-Setting Issues Under the Patent, Copyright, and Antitrust Laws' (2003) 43 IDEA 331, 338; Dr habil Nizar Abdelkaf and others, *Understanding ICT Standardization: Principles and Practice* (ETSI 2018) 20 <www.etsi.org/images/files/Education/Understanding_ICT_Standardization_LoResWeb_20190524.pdf> accessed 1 January 2021.

[13] Joanna Tsai and Joshua D Wright, 'Standard setting, Intellectual Property Rights, and the Role of Antitrust in regulating incomplete contracts' (2015) 80 Antitrust Law Journal 157, 159.

[14] Dr habil Nizar Abdelkaf and others, *Understanding ICT Standardization: Principles and Practice* (ETSI 2018) 15 <www.etsi.org/images/files/Education/Understanding_ICT_Standardization_LoResWeb_20190524.pdf> accessed 1 January 2021.

[15] Ibid.

[16] Ibid.

[17] Bruce H Kobayashi and Joshua D Wright, 'Intellectual Property and Standard Setting' George Mason Law & Economics Research Paper No. 09-40, 3.

[18] Patrick D Curran, 'Standard-Setting Organizations: Patents, Price Fixing, and Per Se Legality' (2003) 70(3) The University of Chicago Law Review 983, 986; Alexei Alexandrov, 'Anti-competitive interconnection: the effects of the elasticity of consumers' expectations and the shape of the network effects function' (2012) NET Institute Working Paper No. 08-07.

On the other hand, as a downside, standards, especially technology standards, can also affect further innovation.[19] It has been suggested that it is difficult to change or evolve where there exists an obligation to follow an existing standard.[20] Further, the steps followed during the adoption of a new standard are quite complex.[21]

3 Standard Setting Organizations

The number of technical specifications and their development process would decide the composition and functioning of an SSO. Therefore, it is challenging to ascertain a uniform definition; however, SSOs are "… primarily engaged in activities such as developing, coordinating, promulgating, revising, amending, reissuing, interpreting, or otherwise maintaining hundreds of thousands of standards applicable to a wide base of users outside the standards developing organization".[22] One can only describe an SSO based on the role it adopts in developing a technology standard. Over the years, many have tried describing SSOs as certification agents, as places where technology bargaining happens, thereby facilitating consensual licensing, and places that provide an opportunity for joint R&D.[23] Broadly, they provide a platform where different stakeholders can provide their inputs while formalizing and operationalizing a particular standard or standards.

A report published for the European Commission in 2014 has categorized standard bodies into three categories: (i) formally recognized, (ii) quasi-formal, and (iii) privately organized consortia. The first category includes those SSOs recognized by regulatory organizations and are further sub-divided territorially as global, regional, and national. Examples are the International Organization for Standardization (ISO) and the European Telecommunications Standards Institute (ETSI). Those coming under the 'quasi-formal' group without having an outright formal recognition have received comparable recognition due to donning some of the characteristics of formally recognized standard bodies. Examples are the Institute of Electrical and

---

[19] Dr habil Nizar Abdelkaf and others, *Understanding ICT Standardization: Principles and Practice* (ETSI 2018) 20 <www.etsi.org/images/files/Education/Understanding_ICT_Standardization_LoR esWeb_20190524.pdf> accessed 1 January 2021.

[20] Ibid.

[21] Ibid.

[22] US Legal, 'Standard Setting Organization [SSO]' (Law & Legal Definition, US Legal) <http://definitions.uslegal.com/s/standard-setting-organization-sso/> accessed 1 January 2021.

[23] Timothy Simcoe, 'Governing the Anticommons: Institutional Design for Standard-Setting Organizations' (2014) 14(1) Innovation Policy and the Economy 99, 100; L Cabral and D Salant, 'Evolving Technologies and Standards Regulation' (2014) 36 48; J Farrell and T Simcoe, 'Choosing the Rules for Consensus Standardization' (2012) 43(2) The RAND Journal of Economics 235; Mark A. Lemley, 'Intellectual Property Rights and Standard-Setting Organizations' (2002) 90 California Law Review 1889; J Lerner and J Tirole, 'A Model of Forum Shopping' (2006) 96(4) American Economic Review 1091; T Simcoe, 'Standard Setting Committees: Consensus Governance for Shared Technology Platforms' (2012) 102(1) American Economic Review 305.

Electronics Engineers (IEEE) Standards Association and the Internet Engineering Task Force (IETF). Smaller, private consortia would come under the third category.[24]

Individuals representing firms active in a relevant technology often play a leading role in developing a standard in a standard setting body.[25] There is also the involvement of academics and participants representing different governments and other interested parties.[26] The role played by all participants in SSOs is voluntary, including their subsequent compliance with an adopted technology standard.[27] Membership forms for two of the three SSOs considered in this chapter have been shared in the annexure.[28]

There is no consistency in how existing literature has used SSO and a Standard Development Organization (SDO).[29] It has been suggested that the two terms differ "from an economics and resource allocation perspective" because "setting standards" and "developing standards" are inherently different.[30] Arguably, the word ""standard

---

[24] RNA Bekkers and others, 'Patents and standards: a modern framework for IPR-based standardisation' (European Commission 2014) 31 <https://doi.org/10.2769/90861> accessed 1 January 2021; Jorge L Contreras, 'Technical Standards, Standards-Setting Organizations and Intellectual Property: A Survey of the Literature (With an Emphasis on Empirical Approaches)' in Peter S. Menell and David Schwartz (eds), *Research Handbooks on the Economics of Intellectual Property Law, Vol 2 - Analytical Methods* (Edward Elgar 2019).

[25] 'Technical Standards, Standards-Setting Organizations and Intellectual Property: A Survey of the Literature (With an Emphasis on Empirical Approaches)' in Peter S. Menell and David Schwartz (eds), *Research Handbooks on the Economics of Intellectual Property Law, Vol 2 - Analytical Methods* (Edward Elgar 2019).

[26] Ibid.; Justus Baron and Daniel F Spulber, 'Technology Standards and Standard Setting Organizations: Introduction to the Searle Center Database' (2018) Northwestern Law & Econ Research Paper No. 17-16, 28.

[27] Justus Baron and Daniel F Spulber, 'Technology Standards and Standard Setting Organizations: Introduction to the Searle Center Database' (2018) Northwestern Law & Econ Research Paper No. 17-16, 6.

[28] The membership forms of TSDSI and ETSI have are shared as Annexure I and VI respectively.

[29] Dr habil Nizar Abdelkaf and others, *Understanding ICT Standardization: Principles and Practice* (ETSI 2018) 23 <www.etsi.org/images/files/Education/Understanding_ICT_Standardization_LoResWeb_20190524.pdf> accessed 1 January 2021; Justus Baron and others, 'Making the rules. The Governance of Standard Development Organizations and their Policies on Intellectual Property Rights' (Publications Office of the European Union 2019) 24 <https://publications.jrc.ec.eur opa.eu/repository/bitstream/JRC115004/sdo_governance_final_electronic_version.pdf> accessed 1 January 2021; Jorge L Contreras, 'Technical Standards, Standards-Setting Organizations and Intellectual Property: A Survey of the Literature (With an Emphasis on Empirical Approaches)' in Peter S. Menell and David Schwartz (eds), *Research Handbooks on the Economics of Intellectual Property Law, Vol 2 - Analytical Methods* (Edward Elgar 2019); David J Teece and Edward F Sherry, 'Standards Setting, Standards Development and Division of the Gains from Standardization' (Competition Policy International 2016) <https://www.competitionpolicyinternational.com/standards-set ting-standards-development-and-division-of-the-gains-from-standardization/> accessed 1 January 2021.

[30] David J Teece and Edward F Sherry, 'Standards Setting, Standards Development and Division of the Gains from Standardization' (Competition Policy International 2016) <https://www.compet itionpolicyinternational.com/standards-setting-standards-development-and-division-of-the-gains-from-standardization/> accessed 1 January 2021.

setting" is used for activities at the lower end of the spectrum, and "standard development" is used for activities at the higher end of the spectrum."[31] SSO is a broad umbrella term encompassing multilateral organizations that facilitate standard setting processes such as Special Interest Groups (SIGs), SDOs, consortia, and other entities.[32] For this book, we are going to use SSO. Due to the different nature of the group that forms an SSO, SSOs cannot have a unique internal structure. Therefore, their legal liability would be different as well.[33] IEEE is instituted under the New York Not-For-Profit Corporation Law, whereas ETSI has been incorporated under the French Law.[34] TSDSI, on the other hand, is a not-for-profit autonomous organization under the Indian Societies Registration Act.[35]

4 Importance of SSOs in Setting Essential Patents

SSOs play a leading role in developing technology standards. With different participants, the internal process structures are different for different SSOs, although there is a broad range of similarities irrespective of the size of an SSO. While there are multiple advantages, there are often questions connected to the adverse outcomes of a standard setting process.

4.1 Standard Setting Process in SSOs

SSO members accept a particular standard by following an elaborate process. The work starts with the deliberation of a group of experts concerning a proposed standard within an SSO.[36] The internal rules of an SSO will govern the exact nature of the process to be followed while creating the standard.[37] As a general rule, an SSO creates

---

[31] Ibid.

[32] Timothy Simcoe, 'Governing the Anticommons: Institutional Design for Standard-Setting Organizations' (2014) 14(1) Innovation Policy and the Economy 99, 103; Jurgita Randakeviciūte, 'Chapter SSOs and their functions in Standardization' in *The Role of Standard-Setting Organizations with regard to balancing the rights between the owners and the users of standard-essential patent* (2015) 18.

[33] Andrew Updegrove, 'Chapter 6: Forming A Successful Consortium Part II—Legal Considerations' (ConsortiumInfo.com) <https://www.consortiuminfo.org/essentialguide/forming2.php> accessed 10 November 2020.

[34] IEEE, 'Tax and Corporate Information' <https://www.ieee.org/about/help/business-policies/tax-corporate-info.html> accessed 1 January 2021; ETSI, 'About Us' <https://www.etsi.org/technologies/14-about> accessed 1 January 2021.

[35] TSDSI, 'Overview of TSDSI' <https://tsdsi.in/about/> accessed 1 January 2021.

[36] OECD Policy Roundtables, OECD Policy Roundtables, 'Standard Setting' 2010 DAF/COMP (2010) 33, 25 <www.oecd.org/daf/competition/47381304.pdf> accessed 1 January 2021.

[37] OECD Policy Roundtables, OECD Policy Roundtables, 'Standard Setting' 2010 DAF/COMP (2010) 33, 25 <www.oecd.org/daf/competition/47381304.pdf> accessed 1 January 2021.

rules for stakeholders about the process of standard setting, voting on standardization decisions, and making technological contributions.[38] The rules concern questions about:

- Those who are eligible to vote and provide input on new or revised standards
- Development of standard and the formal steps to be followed
- Release of information about essential IPs
- Required consensus for fixing a standard.[39]

SSOs generally have an overarching technology theme and work on issues connected to that theme.[40] The participants of an SSO, including but not limited to firms, universities, government, individuals, and public interest groups[41] at the initial stage, can submit technical proposals relating to the standards that are being developed. Once submitted, various working groups review these technical proposals.[42] There are multiple working groups comprised of engineers and other technical experts in an SSO that focus on particular technical issues connected to the theme.[43] It is up to these working groups to determine the best technologies available to implement the relevant standard. The entire process is lengthy and involves a series of collaborative and iterative discussions, and they may accept, reject, and even seek changes to the submitted technology proposals.[44] The merits and demerits of the recommendations are discussed over several meetings organized by the working groups. To reach a consensus, they conduct several meetings among attendees to discuss the merits and demerits of the proposed technology related to a particular standard.[45]

With different standard setting processes at different SSOs, there is a broad framework that any SSO is likely to follow. Figure 1 is an illustration of the overall framework suggested in the ETSI report published in 2018.

---

[38] Justus Baron and others, 'Making the rules. The Governance of Standard Development Organizations and their Policies on Intellectual Property Rights' (Publications Office of the European Union 2019) 11 <https://publications.jrc.ec.europa.eu/repository/bitstream/JRC115004/sdo_governance_final_electronic_version.pdf> accessed 1 January 2021.

[39] OECD Policy Roundtables, OECD Policy Roundtables, 'Standard Setting' 2010 DAF/COMP (2010) 33, 25 <www.oecd.org/daf/competition/47381304.pdf> accessed 1 January 2021.

[40] Kristen Jakobsen Osenga, 'Ignorance Over Innovation: Why Misunderstanding Standard Setting Organizations Will Hinder Technological Progress' (2018) 56 U Louisville Law Review 159, 179.

[41] Andrew Updegrove, 'Chapter 1: What (and Why) is an SSO?' (consortiuminfo.org) <https://www.consortiuminfo.org/essentialguide/whatisansso.php> accessed 1 January 2021.

[42] Kristen Jakobsen Osenga, 'Ignorance Over Innovation: Why Misunderstanding Standard Setting Organizations Will Hinder Technological Progress' (2018) 56 U Louisville Law Review 159, 180.

[43] Daniel S Sternberg, 'A Brief History of Rand' (2014) 20(2) Boston University Journal of Science and Technology Law 211, 213.

[44] Justus Baron and Kirti Gupta, 'Unpacking 3GPP Standards' (2018) 27(3) Journal of Economics & Management Strategy 433.

[45] Kirti Gupta, 'Technology Standards and Competition in the Mobile Wireless Industry' (2015) 22 Geo Mason Law Review 865, 571.

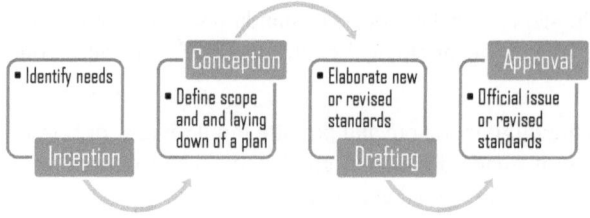

Fig. 1 Standard setting process[46]

At the stage of inception, the idea of identifying the need for a new standard begins. It is followed by initiating the process of standardization. A detailed plan is laid out before an SSO conceptualizes beyond the technical proposal. It includes planning the organization's time schedule, setting the target outcomes, and deciding how relevant resources are directed toward implementing the plan.[47] During the drafting phase, the technical and editorial work is carried out according to the internal rules that create a mature and stable document before it is released officially.[48] The last phase is the approval phase wherein consensus is sought. If the approval process's outcome is negative, the document may return to the drafting phase.[49] Once the standard is agreed upon and the consensus is reached among the participants, there are further licensing issues. The issues of licensing are an integral part of the IPR policies of SSOs.

4.2   Advantages and Risk of Standard Setting by SSOs

Various participants of an SSO stand to benefit from the process of standard setting and the position of having a standard in place. It depends on the role that they would play in an SSO.[50] With the available opportunity to submit technical proposals toward the standard setting, participants can actively develop a standard. Therefore, depending on their contribution, participants can lead the process of standard setting.[51] A contributor to the technology will benefit from licensing once a patent becomes part of that technology, i.e., an essential patent in a standard essential patent.

---

[46] Dr habil Nizar Abdelkaf and others, *Understanding ICT Standardization: Principles and Practice* (ETSI 2018) 32 <www.etsi.org/images/files/Education/Understanding_ICT_Standardization_LoR esWeb_20190524.pdf> accessed 1 January 2021.

[47] Ibid.

[48] Ibid.

[49] Ibid.

[50] Kristen Jakobsen Osenga, 'Ignorance Over Innovation: Why Misunderstanding Standard Setting Organizations Will Hinder Technological Progress' (2018) 56 U Louisville Law Review 159, 166.

[51] Andrew Updegrove, 'Chapter 2: Participating In Standard Setting Organizations: Value Propositions, Roles And Strategies' <https://www.consortiuminfo.org/essentialguide/participating1.php> accessed 1 January 2021.

A participant looking to use the standard and, therefore, the technology can incorporate it in the developed product at an early stage.[52] It reduces future hassle for the implementer and, thus, the cost.

Furthermore, it is always tricky to engage in developing a new standard independently.[53] The process of standardization entails horizontal competition since participants can freely compete to incorporate their technology into a particular standard.[54] It encourages participants to innovate and market their products to the consumers at a competitive rate. Consumers can shift from one product to another, complying with the same adopted standard. It gives freedom in terms of the price of a product and choice of product.[55] The development of a standard at an SSO has additional advantages over market determined standards. It avoids possible complications while adopting an already developed standard. Further, it may defeat the purpose of interoperability and interconnectivity, which you would expect from a technology standard.[56]

Standardization at SSOs also brings about several challenges. In the last several decades, their IPR policies have increasingly played a crucial role in private litigation and have attracted scrutiny from policymakers and regulators.[57] The contradictions are between innovators on the one hand and implementers on the other. Innovators would seek to maximize their investment toward developing a technology standard. Implementers would like to use such technology in the accepted standard on reasonable terms.[58]

Patent hold-up and Patent hold-out are two different situations that have been debated intensely. As the name suggests, hold-up arguably happens because the innovator's control over the use of essential patents in a technology ties up further

---

[52] Andrew Updegrove, 'Chapter 2: Participating In Standard Setting Organizations: Value Propositions, Roles And Strategies' <https://www.consortiuminfo.org/essentialguide/participating1.php> accessed 1 January 2021; Robert L. Stoll, 'What you should know about US Standard-Essential Patents' (Law360 2013) <https://www.law360.com/articles/472229/what-you-should-know-about-us-standard-essential-patents>.

[53] Ibid.; Joshua D. Wright, 'SSOs, FRAND, and Antitrust: Lessons from the Economics of Incomplete Contracts' (2014) 21 Geo. Mason Law Review 791, 793.

[54] Benjamin M Miller, 'FRAND-Encumbered SEPs and Injunctions: Why Section 5 of the FTC Act is an inappropriate remedy', (2015) 16 Columbia Science and Technology Law Review 452, 460.

[55] Joshua D. Wright, 'SSOs, FRAND, and Antitrust: Lessons from the Economics of Incomplete Contracts' (2014) 21 Geo Mason Law Review 791, 793.

[56] Kristen Jakobsen Osenga, 'Ignorance Over Innovation: Why Misunderstanding Standard Setting Organizations Will Hinder Technological Progress' (2018) 56 U Louisville Law Review 159, 166; Joanna Tsai and Joshua D Wright, 'Standard setting, Intellectual Property Rights, and the Role of Antitrust in regulating incomplete contracts' (2015) 80 Antitrust Law Journal 157, 160.

[57] Kirti Gupta, 'FRAND in India: Emerging Developments' (2018) 30 (1) IIBM Management Review 27; Jorge L Contreras, 'Technical Standards, Standards-Setting Organizations and Intellectual Property: A Survey of the Literature (With an Emphasis on Empirical Approaches)' in Peter S. Menell and David Schwartz (eds), *Research Handbooks on the Economics of Intellectual Property Law, Vol 2 - Analytical Methods* (Edward Elgar 2019).

[58] Pierre Larouche and Geertrui Van Overwalle, 'Interoperability Standards, Patents and Competition Policy' (2014) TILEC Discussion Paper 2014-050 5.

implementers.[59] The fear is that innovators would charge exorbitant royalty and not necessarily FRAND (Fair, Reasonable, and Non-Discriminatory) terms as agreed upon under SSO IPR policies.[60] Literature suggests that there is no empirical evidence suggesting the existence of hold-up.[61] Hold-out represents a possibility where an innovator is deprived of royalty by an implementer. In this situation, implementers can adopt delaying tactics after an innovator has incurred costs over the invention.[62] The obligation is not only on the SEP holder but equally on the implementer. There are other concerns like royalty stacking and patent ambush. Royalty stacking is when an implementer must pay royalties to more than one patent holder due to the use of multiple essential patents in a standard. It may lead to increasing the cost of the end product.[63] Again, the absence of empirical evidence has been cited against the idea of patent ambush.[64]

Participants playing a leading role in developing a technology standard will play an equally important role in disclosing their essential patents used in such a standard and subsequent licensing to implementers. The disclosure and licensing process are facilitated by IPR policies of different SSOs, leading to the successful implementation of the standards. These policies will be discussed in much greater detail in the subsequent sections. Participants of SSOs, wherever applicable, voluntarily pledge patents that are considered essential to the development of a standard. Further, they agree to work according to the IPR policies of the SSOs.[65]

---

[59] Joanna Tsai and Joshua D Wright, 'Standard setting, Intellectual Property Rights, and the Role of Antitrust in regulating incomplete contracts' (2015) 80 Antitrust Law Journal 157.

[60] Ibid.

[61] Kirti Gupta, 'FRAND in India: Emerging Developments' (2018) 30 (1) IIBM Management Review 27; Anne Layne-Farrar, 'Why Patent Holdout is Not Just a Fancy Name for Plain Old Patent Infringement' (Competition Policy International CPI 2016) <https://www.competitionpoli cyinternational.com/why-patent-holdout-is-not-just-a-fancy-name-for-plain-old-patent-infringem ent/> accessed 1 January 2021.

[62] Jorge L Contreras, 'Technical Standards, Standards-Setting Organizations and Intellectual Property: A Survey of the Literature (With an Emphasis on Empirical Approaches)' in Peter S. Menell and David Schwartz (eds), *Research Handbooks on the Economics of Intellectual Property Law, Vol 2 - Analytical Methods* (Edward Elgar 2019).

[63] Mark A. Lemley and Carl Shapiro, 'Patent Holdup and Royalty Stacking' (2007) 85 Texas Law Review 1991.

[64] J Gregory Sidak, 'The Antitrust Division's Devaluation of Standard Essential Patents' (2015) 14 Georgetown Law Journal Online 48.

[65] Jindal Initiative on Research in IP and Competition (JIRICO), 'Response to the questions raised in the discussion paper released by DIPP' (2016) Response to question b <https://jgu.edu.in/jirico/ pdf/DIPP_response_FINAL.PDF> accessed 1 January 2021.

4.3 IPR Policies of SSOs: Understanding Disclosure and Licensing of Essential Patents

The SSO IPR policies are drafted to address the concern of the technology provider and the concern of the implementer who would rely on such a technology. However, it is not an easy process to reconcile between those who rightfully expect to commercialize their essential patents incorporated in a standard with those hoping to use those essential patents lawfully.[66] Therefore, SSO IPR policies are situated at the cusp of rival interests.[67] While most SSOs have adopted a comprehensive set of internal rules adhered to by all participants, the rules about disclosure of essential patents and licensing of those patents have attracted considerable debate.[68] They are also the two most important obligations that SSOs impose on the patent holders.[69]

Over time the IPR policies at SSOs do change, at times yearly amendments and adaptations take place.[70] However, unlike today, the initial SSO policies were not thought out documents, and they had to undergo significant revisions.[71] At times, changes happened as a subsequent event to prominent litigations.[72] Surveys point out that only some of the changes out of the many would be considered substantial.[73] For instance, the decision in *Rambus* arguably led to the tightening of the patent disclosure policies.[74] For the purpose of the chapter, we have considered the SSO IPR policies of ETSI, IEEE, and TSDI with a particular reference to disclosure and subsequent licensing of essential patents.

---

[66] George S Cary and others, 'The case for antitrust law to police the patent holdup problem in standard setting' (2011) 77 Antitrust Law Journal No 3 913, 915.

[67] National Research Council, *Patent Challenges for Standard-Setting in the Global Economy: Lessons from Information and Communications Technology* (The National Academies Press 2013) 4, 16; Patent Challenges for Standard-Setting in the Global Economy; Joseph Farell and others, 'Standard setting, patents and hold-up' (2007) 74 Antitrust Law Journal No. 3 603, 646.

[68] Rudi Bekkers, 'Disclosure Rules and Declared Essential Patents' (2017) <http://people.bu.edu/tsimcoe/documents/working/dSEP7.pdf> accessed 18 January 2021; RNA Bekkers and others, 'Patents and standards: a modern framework for IPR-based standardisation' (European Commission 2014) 41 <https://doi.org/10.2769/90861> accessed 1 January 2021.

[69] Haris Tsilikas, *Antitrust Enforcement and Standard Essential Patents: Moving beyond the FRAND Commitment* (Nomos Verlagsgesellschaft mbH 2017) 26.

[70] J Tsai and J Wright, 'Standard Setting, Intellectual Property Rights, and the Role of Antitrust in Regulating Incomplete Contracts' (2015) 80 Antitrust Law Journal No 1 157, 170.

[71] Kraig A Jakobsen, 'Revisiting Standard-Setting Organizations' Patent Policies' (2004) 3 Nw J Tech & Intell Prop 43, 49.

[72] Jorge L. Contreras, 'Technical Standards, Standards-Setting Organizations and Intellectual Property: A Survey of the Literature (With an Emphasis on Empirical Approaches)' in Peter S. Menell and David Schwartz (eds), *Research Handbooks on the Economics of Intellectual Property Law, Vol 2 - Analytical Methods* (Edward Elgar, 2019-Forthcoming).

[73] Justus Baron and others, 'Making the rules. The Governance of Standard Development Organizations and their Policies on Intellectual Property Rights' (Publications Office of the European Union 2019) 137 <https://publications.jrc.ec.europa.eu/repository/bitstream/JRC115004/sdo_governance_final_electronic_version.pdf> accessed 1 January 2021.

[74] Ibid. at 140.

To begin with, it is essential to understand the concept of essential patents. The concept of essentiality has been approached in two different ways—when there are no technological alternatives and instances where there may be alternatives, but they are too expensive, leading to commercial essentiality.[75] Broadly, "… essentiality is defined with respect to patents necessary for implementing the final standard."[76] While the development process can consider many patents as essential, only "ultimately necessary" patents will be considered for licensing.[77] Following essentiality, SSOs expect members who contribute to the development of a standard to disclose essential patents and license those patents in a FRAND manner.[78]

5 Disclosure and Licensing of Essential Patents

Disclosure, a compliance process in nature, ensures that the information about essential patents is reasonably known to those technology users. The scope and understanding of disclosure are broad, with the following questions:

> Whose patents must be disclosed; what qualifies as an "essential" patent or patent claim; when disclosures must be made in the standards development process; whether blanket (non-patent specific) disclosures suffice; to whom the disclosed information is provided; and whether there is a requirement to update disclosures, for example, as a standard evolves and as patents are issued or denied.[79]

The disclosure process ensures transparency, and members adopting a standard with essential patents are informed beforehand about their various commercial liabilities.[80] In the words of the European Commission, transparency entails, "… the relevant standard-setting organisation would need to have procedures which allow stakeholders to effectively inform themselves of upcoming, on-going and finalised standardisation work in good time at each stage of the development of the standard."[81] There is a general consensus about prior disclosures for future patent claims concerning a standard so that participants are informed at the time of voting on a

---

[75] National Research Council, *Patent Challenges for Standard-Setting in the Global Economy: Lessons from Information and Communications Technology* (The National Academies Press 2013) 38.

[76] Ibid. at 39.

[77] Ibid.

[78] National Research Council, *Patent Challenges for Standard-Setting in the Global Economy: Lessons from Information and Communications Technology* (The National Academies Press 2013) 17.

[79] Ibid. at 4.

[80] Haris Tsilikas, *Antitrust Enforcement and Standard Essential Patents: Moving beyond the FRAND Commitment* (Nomos Verlagsgesellschaft mbH 2017) 15.

[81] European Commission, 'Guidelines on the applicability of Article 101 of the Treaty on the Functioning of the European Union to horizontal co-operation agreements' [2011] OJ C11/1.

technical specification.[82] The disclosure requirement helps implementers willing to license SEPs on FRAND terms. It also reduces claims about deceptive conduct and 'patent ambush.'[83] SSO policies suggest patent disclosures in different ways.[84] The processes of disclosing essential patents and the timing, knowledge, level of detail, and definition of essentiality and updating each one varies greatly. While there is a requirement of disclosure, there is no uniformity across SSOs as to the extent and time of such disclosure of essential patents.[85] An example of an IPR disclosure form relevant to a proposed standard has been shared in the annexure.[86]

Discovering essentiality during the development of the standard is an arduous task for those with multiple patent portfolios. There is no ideal time for declaring essentiality, and further, those likely to have multiple essential patents may not want to entail a cost-intensive patent search to identify such patents.[87] SSOs do not require patent holders to carry out patent searches mandatorily.[88] The difficulty is limited to cost and the fact that it is challenging to predict essentiality at the stage of development, especially at an early stage.[89] Similarly, disclosing late when the standard has matured may come as a surprise for the SSO members.[90] The overall effect could be possible overdisclosure and underdisclosure from the side of the patent holder. There could be a situation where there is a general declaration by a technology holder and instances where specific patents are declared.[91] These sorts of declarations are known as generic or blanket disclosures.[92] While these are existing rationales for different kinds of disclosures provided by the essential patent holders, there is an additional fear that any specific declaration of an essential patent may attract antitrust claims. A specific declaration may lead others to believe that there

---

[82] Robert A Skitol, 'Concerted buying power: its potential for addressing the patent holdup problem in standard setting' (2005) 72(2) Antitrust Law Journal 727, 730.

[83] Haris Tsilikas, *Antitrust Enforcement and Standard Essential Patents: Moving beyond the FRAND Commitment* (Nomos Verlagsgesellschaft mbH 2017) 26.

[84] Robert A Skitol, 'Concerted buying power: its potential for addressing the patent holdup problem in standard setting' (2005) 72(2) Antitrust Law Journal 727, 732.

[85] National Research Council, *Patent Challenges for Standard-Setting in the Global Economy: Lessons from Information and Communications Technology* (The National Academies Press 2013) 40.

[86] The IPR disclosure form of TSDSI are attached as Annexure II–V.

[87] National Research Council, *Patent Challenges for Standard-Setting in the Global Economy: Lessons from Information and Communications Technology* (The National Academies Press 2013) 41.

[88] Jindal Initiative on Research in IP and Competition (JIRICO), 'Response to the questions raised in the discussion paper released by DIPP' (2016) Response to question b <https://jgu.edu.in/jirico/pdf/DIPP_response_FINAL.PDF> accessed 5 January 2021.

[89] National Research Council, *Patent Challenges for Standard-Setting in the Global Economy: Lessons from Information and Communications Technology* (The National Academies Press 2013) 42.

[90] Ibid.

[91] Josh Lerner, Haris Tabakovic and Jean Tirole, 'Patent Disclosures and Standard-Setting' (2016) NBER Working Paper No. w22768 3.

[92] Ibid.

are no further essential patents from the patent owner. A late realization on a patent owner's part about a missing essential patent, even though inadvertently, can make the patent owner vulnerable.[93] While specific disclosure has certain disadvantages, a patent owner may still want to opt for it when a patent is undoubtedly valuable for the standard's purpose.[94] On the other hand, a declaration of too many patents as essential for a standard may be construed as an impediment to the standard setting process.[95] In the end, disclosure could end the uncertainty that users of technology may have and help inventors collect their licensing fees.[96]

Licensing rules entail that an essential patent holder commit to give away the technology through licensing to downstream implementers who would use such technology for manufacturing products. The SSO IPR policies are geared toward ensuring that all SEP licenses are made further available to all those who would require the technology. SSOs have adopted mechanisms like Licensing Statements, Undertakings, Letters of Assurance, and Declarations of Licensing Position to shape this vision.[97] FRAND is an optimal licensing commitment, which reflects in SSOs policy documents. Following the FRAND, an owner of essential patents in a standard promises to enter into good faith negotiations and extend a license to an implementer in a downstream market. FRAND, in the last decade or so, has been the reason for most litigations. Beyond mentioning FRAND in their IPR policies, SSOs have left the meaning to be ascertained through bilateral negotiations of parties involved or through judgements of Courts in different jurisdictions.[98] FRAND draws the patent holder and implementer closer to a system that may not always have started on equal footing. It should help both parties involved in a FRAND transaction, but the efficacy of FRAND will only be determined by enforceability.[99]

SSOs majorly started to frame their policies in the 1990s; however, SSOs' more proactive behavior has been noticed with the emergence of 2G mobile telecommunication standard and upon the insistence of Competition Authorities in Europe.[100]

---

[93] Josh Lerner, Haris Tabakovic and Jean Tirole, 'Patent Disclosures and Standard-Setting' (2016) NBER Working Paper No. w22768 6.

[94] Ibid.

[95] Ibid. at 7; R Bekkers and others, 'Standardizing intellectual property disclosure data' (2011) 7 <https://pure.tue.nl/ws/portalfiles/portal/57881074/387600165841283.pdf> accessed 18 January 2021.

[96] Benjamin Chiao, Josh Lerner and Jean Tirole, 'The Rules of Standard-Setting Organizations: An Empirical Analysis' (2007) 38(4) The RAND Journal of Economics 905.

[97] Rudi Bekkers and Andrew Updegrove, 'A study of IPR policies and practices of a representative group of Standards Setting Organizations worldwide' <https://doi.org/10.2139/ssrn.2333445>.

[98] RNA Bekkers and others, 'Patents and standards: a modern framework for IPR-based standardisation' (European Commission 2014) 31 <https://doi.org/10.2769/90861> accessed 18 January 2021.

[99] DIPP, 'Discussion Paper on Standard Essential Patents and their Availability on FRAND terms' (1 March 2016) <http://dipp.nic.in/sites/default/files/standardEssentialPaper_01March2016_0.pdf> accessed 18 January 2021.

[100] E Iversen, 'Standardization and Intellectual Property Rights (IPR): ETSI's controversial search for new policies' IEEE conference on Standardization and Innovation in Information Technology' (1999) <https://eprints.utas.edu.au/1297/1/Iversen_ETSI_2OO2.pdf> accessed 18 January 2021.

The Communication of 1992, published by the European Commission on Intellectual Property Rights and Standardization[101]: "sets out a number of [general] principles[102] which it believes should form the basis of any internal rules which standards bodies may wish to elaborate."[103] Some of the principles that reflect in SSO IPR policies ensure that

> ... standards are available for use on fair, reasonable and non-discriminatory terms, regardless of whether the users participate in the work of the standard-making body or not, but taking into account the circumstances of the use; [and] fair conditions are provided to the holders of intellectual property rights, especially concerning the time limits for identifying IPRs and agreeing to their use, and in respect of arbitration mechanisms as to royalty rates.[104]

The essential patent holders should "... use best efforts to identify in a timely manner any IPR which they hold which is relevant to a standard which is being developed and to confirm or refuse permission for its incorporation in that standard promptly; [and] offer fair, reasonable and non-discriminatory monetary or non-monetary terms for the licence[e] to use any IPR."[105] The disclosure and licensing provisions of the three SSOs—IEEE, ETSI, and TSDSI—have been discussed.

5.1 Disclosure and Licensing Requirements ETSI

The IPR Policy of ETSI has seen several changes over the years following the norm that SSOs had to undergo in their policies. These changes have happened due to concerns related to a possible holding-up situation that arguably essential patent owners may indulge in and antitrust concerns raised by the European Commission at different times.[106] For instance, one of the policy changes required the essential patent holders to offer FRAND licenses to members regarding current and future ETSI standards. It was not extended to non-members not part of ETSI, leading to an investigation by the EC.[107] There have been concerns about the disclosure

---

[101] European Commission, 'Intellectual Property Rights and Standardization' COM (92) 445 final.

[102] Ibid., Section 6.2.1.

[103] Ibid., Section 1.1.2.

[104] Ibid., Section 6.2.1.

[105] Ibid.

[106] 1993 policy changes have been suggested resulted due to possible hold-up situation; Jorge Contreras, 'Technical Standards, Standards-Setting Organizations and Intellectual Property: A Survey of the Literature (with an Emphasis on Empirical Approaches)' in Peter S. Menell & David Schwartz (eds) Research Handbooks on the Economics of Intellectual Property Law: Analytical Methods (Edward Elgar 2017) 3.

[107] Jorge Contreras, 'Technical Standards, Standards-Setting Organizations and Intellectual Property: A Survey of the Literature (with an Emphasis on Empirical Approaches)' in Peter S. Menell & David Schwartz (eds) Research Handbooks on the Economics of Intellectual Property Law: Analytical Methods (Edward Elgar 2017); Maurits Dolmans, Standards for Standards (2002) 26 FORDHAM INTL. LJ. 163, 181.

obligations under the existing policy leading to a further investigation in 2005 by the Commission, which again was addressed by a policy change.[108]

Likewise, in 2007, a shift from an ex ante licensing Disclosure was adopted in 2006 to a voluntary licensing ex ante disclosure. Upon the Commission's intervention, the policy that suggested splitting of royalty patents in advance among patent holders in a proportional manner was dropped.[109]

The present IPR policy on Disclosure of IPRs put the onus on members to

> ... use its reasonable endeavours, in particular during the development of a [standard] or [technical specification] where it participates, to inform ETSI of [essential] IPRs in a timely [manner]. In particular, a [member] submitting a technical proposal for a [standard] or [technical specification] shall, on a bona fide basis, draw the attention of ETSI to any of that [member's] IPR which might be [essential] if that proposal is adopted.[110]

There is, however, no "... obligation on MEMBERS to conduct IPR searches."[111]

The disclosure policy adopted by ETSI requires its members to fulfil four conditions. There is a component of good faith on the patent holder's part since the policy expects the patent holder to use 'reasonable endeavours' and engage in 'bonafide' transactions without any intention to deceive the other party. Lord Mansfield in *Carter v Boehm* said, "good faith forbids either party by concealing what he privately knows, to draw the other into a bargain, from his ignorance of that fact and his believing the contrary."[112] A member promptly must inform ETSI about an essential IPR in a standard. The onus is higher when a member submits a technical proposal toward developing the standard and sharing the information about a patent that may be deemed essential upon the acceptance of a standard. While there are reasonable expectations for members to disclose, they are not expected to carry out patent searches to understand a particular standard's essentiality.

Following the disclosure policy, ETSI has drawn up its policy for licensing commitments regarding essential patents.[113] After identifying the essential IPR about a particular standard or a technical specification, "... the Director-General of ETSI shall immediately request the owner to give within three months an irrevocable

---

[108] Jorge Contreras, 'Technical Standards, Standards-Setting Organizations and Intellectual Property: A Survey of the Literature (with an Emphasis on Empirical Approaches)' in Peter S. Menell & David Schwartz (eds) *Research Handbooks on the Economics of Intellectual Property Law: Analytical Methods* (Edward Elgar 2017).

[109] Jorge Contreras, 'Technical Standards, Standards-Setting Organizations and Intellectual Property: A Survey of the Literature (with an Emphasis on Empirical Approaches)' in Peter S. Menell & David Schwartz (eds) *Research Handbooks on the Economics of Intellectual Property Law: Analytical Methods* (Edward Elgar 2017).

[110] ETSI, 'Intellectual Property Rights Policy 2020' Clause 4.1 <https://www.etsi.org/images/files/IPR/etsi-ipr-policy.pdf> accessed 18 January 2021.

[111] ETSI, 'Intellectual Property Rights Policy 2020' Clause 4.2 <https://www.etsi.org/images/files/IPR/etsi-ipr-policy.pdf> accessed 18 January 2021.

[112] *Carter v Boehm* [1766] 1 Burr 1905.

[113] ETSI, 'Intellectual Property Rights Policy 2020' Clause 6 <https://www.etsi.org/images/files/IPR/etsi-ipr-policy.pdf> accessed 18 January 2021.

undertaking in writing that it is prepared to grant irrevocable licences on fair, reasonable and non-discriminatory ("FRAND") terms and conditions under such IPR."[114] FRAND, as expected, has not been elaborated upon and resulted in many private litigations. Some of these cases have been talked about in the third chapter.

5.2 Disclosure and Licensing Requirement of TSDSI

The disclosure requirement of TSDSI is quite similar to the requirement drawn under the ETSI policy. Clause 3 of the IPR policy requires its members to make reasonable endeavors to share timely information about essential patents. There is no obligation on the members to carry out an extensive search for essential patents as long as they enter transactions in good faith and in a bonafide manner.[115] "With respect to [affiliates], the [members] may provide Uniform Resource Locators (URL or link), pointing to the disclosures made by such [affiliates] to any other standards body."[116]

The comparable licensing standard commitments of the TSDI standard are similar to the ETSI standard. When an essential patent is identified, the TSDSI shall notify the patent owner to give an irrevocable undertaking within three months. The broad objective is to ask for a FRAND commitment from a patent holder.

5.3 Disclosure and Licensing Requirement IEEE

The IEEE IPR policy has seen significant changes in a little over two decades. In terms of the FRAND rate, IEEE, before 1995, wanted the essential patent holder to make the technology available at a nominal competitive cost.[117] 2015 saw significant policy amendments regarding licensing commitments and limiting the scope of injunctive relief to patent holders against willing licensees.[118] There was an attempt to qualify FRAND and the suggested royalty rate for licensing of essential patents.[119]

---

[114] ETSI, 'Intellectual Property Rights Policy 2020' Clause 6 <https://www.etsi.org/images/files/IPR/etsi-ipr-policy.pdf> accessed 18 January 2021.

[115] TSDSI, 'Revised IPR Policy' Clause 3 2020 <https://tsdsi.in/wp-content/uploads/2020/02/Revised-IPR-Policy.pdf> accessed 18 January 2021.

[116] TSDSI, 'Revised IPR Policy' Clause 3 2020 <https://tsdsi.in/wp-content/uploads/2020/02/Revised-IPR-Policy.pdf> accessed 18 January 2021.

[117] Jorge L. Contreras, 'An Empirical Study of the Effects of Ex Ante Licensing Disclosure Policies on the Development of Voluntary Technical Standards' (2011) NIST GCR 11-934 10.

[118] Chryssoula Pentheroudakis and Justus A Baron, 'Licensing Terms of Standard Essential Patents. A Comprehensive Analysis of Cases' (2017) JRC Science for Policy Report 83 <https://publications.jrc.ec.europa.eu/repository/bitstream/JRC104068/jrc104068%20online.pdf> accessed 18 January 2021.

[119] Nicolo Zingales and Olia Kanevskaia, 'The IEEE-SA patent policy update under the lens of EU competition law' (2016) 12(2–3) European Competition Journal 195.

Further, an amendment sought to waive the right of seeking an injunction for an essential patent against an implementer. The essential patent holder can lay a claim of injunction only after a successful claim of infringement against the unlicensed implementer in the Court of Appeals.[120]

Unlike the ETSI and TSDI, IEEE uses a single form of assurance[121] [Disclosure for other SSOs] and FRAND commitment.[122] A letter of assurance [LOA] has to be provided by a submitter [essential patent holder][123] within a reasonable time and no later than the approval of a Project Authorization Request [PAR] in the standard development process.[124] In a situation where "[an] asserted potential Essential Patent Claim for which licensing assurance cannot be obtained (e.g., an LOA is not provided or the LOA indicates that licensing assurance is not being provided) [the matter] shall be referred to the Patent Committee."[125] In case a submitter becomes aware of the essential patent not mentioned in the LOA "then such Submitter shall submit a Letter of Assurance stating its position regarding enforcement or licensing of such Patent Claims."[126] However, there is no obligation on the patent holder to carry out an essential patent search.[127]

The FRAND licensing commitment encourages a submitter to "make available a license for Essential Patent Claims to an unrestricted number of applicants on a worldwide basis without compensation or under Reasonable Rates, with other reasonable terms and conditions that are demonstrably free of any unfair discrimination ...."[128] The IPR policy raises the question of prohibitive order against the use of essential patents after the FRAND commitment. Here, the essential patent holder is not encouraged to invoke an injunctive order unless "... the implementer fails to participate in, or to comply with the outcome of, an adjudication, including an affirming first-level appellate review."

Clause D of the form requires the Submitter to disclose any patent that has the potential to become an essential patent.[129] The form covers the issue of reasonable rate, and it means "... appropriate compensation to the patent holder for the practice

---

[120] J. Gregory Sidak, 'The meaning of FRAND, Part II: Injunctions' (2015) 11(1) Journal of Competition Law & Economics 201, 204.

[121] IEEE's Letter of Assurance is attached in Annexure X.

[122] IEEE-SA, 'Standards Board Bylaws 2021' Clause 6 <https://standards.ieee.org/content/dam/ieee-standards/standards/web/documents/other/sb_bylaws.pdf> accessed 18 January 2021.

[123] "Submitter" shall mean an individual or an organization that provides a completed Letter of Assurance. A Submitter may or may not hold Essential Patent Claims. "Submitter" shall include all of its Affiliates unless specifically and permissibly excluded.

[124] IEEE-SA, 'Standards Board Bylaws 2021' Clause 6.2 <https://standards.ieee.org/content/dam/ieee-standards/standards/web/documents/other/sb_bylaws.pdf> accessed 18 January 2021.

[125] IEEE-SA, 'Standards Board Bylaws 2021' Clause 6.2 <https://standards.ieee.org/content/dam/ieee-standards/standards/web/documents/other/sb_bylaws.pdf> accessed 18 January 2021.

[126] Ibid.

[127] Ibid.

[128] IEEE's Letter of Assurance is attached in Annexure IX.

[129] Ibid.

of an Essential Patent Claim excluding the value, if any, resulting from the inclusion of that Essential Patent Claim's technology in the IEEE Standard."[130]

6 FRAND Commitment and Injunction

The mention of FRAND raises a question about a patent holder's right to seek an injunction on the same patent, which has been declared essential. With no definite indication of what FRAND construes under the SSO IPR policy, the issue of a reasonable licensing rate will be contentious. There is a scholarly divide on whether a patent holder waives the right after committing FRAND rates following the SSO IPR policy.[131] Nonetheless, the parties are obligated to good faith negotiation when going over terms of licensing of essential patents in a standard.[132] The outcome may well decide the fate of possible injunctive relief against an implementer or a possible violation of the antitrust law against an essential patent holder.[133]

IEEE IPR policy, amended in 2015, excluded a SEP holder through a 'prohibitive order' from seeking an injunctive relief except otherwise under exceptional circumstances.[134] Contrary to the IEEE, the IPR policy of ETSI does not say anything specific about injunctive relief.[135]

SSOs have a rather challenging task at hand, balancing the need for an innovator and subsequent use of proprietary technology. They can reduce information asymmetry and uncertainty, which is possible in an SSO where participants come from different backgrounds. Not all may have the necessary technical expertise to understand the entire standard setting process and licensing issues. On top of that, there are additional complications with non-members who may not have participated in the standard setting process. Therefore, it raises additional responsibility on SSOs to take transparency as the fulcrum of their internal operations. While there is an

---

[130] Ibid.

[131] Mark Lemley, 'Intellectual Property and Standard-Setting Organizations' (2002) 90(6) California Law Review 1889; Damien Geradin and Miguel Rato, 'Can Standard-Setting Lead to Exploitative Abuse: A Dissonant View on Patent Hold-Up, Royalty Stacking and the Meaning of FRAND' (2007) 3 European Competition Journal 101.

[132] Chryssoula Pentheroudakis and Justus A Baron, 'Licensing Terms of Standard Essential Patents. A Comprehensive Analysis of Cases' (2017) JRC Science for Policy Report <https://publications.jrc.ec.europa.eu/repository/bitstream/JRC104068/jrc104068%20online.pdf> accessed 18 January 2021.

[133] Case C-170/13 *Huawei Technologies Co Ltd v ZTE Corp* EU:C:2015:477; *Unwired Planet v Huawei* [2017] EWHC 711; Makan Delrahim, 'Take it to the Limit: Respecting Innovation Incentives in the Application of Antitrust Law' Remarks as Prepared for Delivery at USC Gould School of Law - Application of Competition Policy to Technology and IP Licensing (2017) <https://www.justice.gov/opa/speech/file/1010746/download> accessed 18 January 2021.

[134] IEEE-SA, 'Standards Board Bylaws 2021' <https://standards.ieee.org/content/dam/ieee-standards/standards/web/documents/other/sb_bylaws.pdf> accessed 18 January 2021.

[135] J Gregory Sidak, 'The Meaning of FRAND, Part II: Injunctions' (2015) 11(1) Journal of Competition Law & Economics 201.

overall uniformity, at least in the examples that we have considered in this chapter, ascertaining FRAND commitment remains a thorny issue. The recourse so far has been court judgements, which will be covered in the next chapter.

Chapter 3
Jurisprudence Evolved in Cases Involving Standard Essential Patents

1 Introduction

SSO IPR Policies generally require two specific commitments from members who intend to submit their underlying technology toward standard development process. The undertaking provided by a prospective implementer to an SSO is that it will make full disclosures of the existing patents and any pending patent applications that are relevant toward the standards development process. SSO members pledging patents toward standard development process are also under an obligation to issue licenses to all implementer on fair, reasonable, and non-discriminatory terms.[1] This chapter examines the scope and wider ramifications of the obligations undertaken by the innovators who participate in the standard development process.

2 Disclosure Requirement

Multiple entities tend to submit their technologies toward standard development process, and it is necessary that SSO members are aware of the varied technologies that are subject matters of such a process, more so, if some of them have been patented. Members would also prefer to be informed about instances where patents are pending on relevant technologies. Awareness about granted and pending patents will enable members to assess between alternative technologies that can either work around existing patents or avoid instances of running into patent thickets. Knowledge about patents essential to a standard development will also enable members to an SSO to include or exclude certain technological features in a standard.[2]

---

[1] Gil Ohana & Brad Biddle, The Disclosure of Patents and Licensing Terms in Standards Development *in* Jorge. L. Contreras (eds), *The Cambridge Handbook of Technical Standardization Law: Competition, Antitrust, and Patents* (Cambridge University Press, 2019).

[2] Ibid.

© The Author(s) 2023
V. H. Bharadwaj et al., *Locating Legal Certainty in Patent Licensing*,
https://doi.org/10.1007/978-981-15-0181-4_3

Disclosures are usually made at the time of the standard development process but does not necessarily end after the standard has been developed.[3] However, there are instances wherein granting of patents might take more time or there could be instances where the patent office might require the applicant to modify the scope of the claims in the patent application. This might result in instances wherein there is over declaration (about the scope of the patent) on the part of the implementer during the standard development process or instances wherein the innovator after gaining knowledge during the development process modify the patent application to make it relevant to the declared standard. In both instances, implementers interest could be affected especially with regards to seeking a FRAND encumbered license.

3   Non-disclosure at the Time of Standard Development

Non-compliance with the disclosure requirement has resulted in litigations and complaints of anticompetitive practices between implementers and innovators. One of the earliest cases involved Dell Computers which had withheld patent information that was relevant to the development of standards related to computers. Dell Computers, a member of Video Electronics Standards Association (VESA), withheld information about a patent it owned that was essential toward the development of a standard on VL-bus, that relay information between the 'computer's central processing unit and its peripheral devices'. Dell had obtained a patent in 1991 but did not disclose it to VESA during the development of the standard. Instead, after eight months from the adoption of the standard and incorporation of the technology in nearly 1.4 million computers, Dell started enforcing its patent against implementers of the VL-bus standard.[4] VESA argued that its policies required members to act in good faith and disclose information relevant to the standard being developed. Dell had also agreed to do so during the standard development process. Therefore, if Dell had acted in good faith and disclosed about the patent, members would have adopted a non-proprietary standard that would have reduced the implementers cost. The Federal Trade Commission (FTC) in its consent order stated if "Dell had acted in good faith and informed about the patent conflict during the standard development process, then it would have enabled VESA to adopt a non-proprietary standard. The

---

[3] For instance, the IPR policy of ETSI states that:

> Subject to Clause 4.2 below, each MEMBER shall use its reasonable endeavours, in particular during the development of a STANDARD or TECHNICAL SPECIFICATION where it participates, to inform ETSI of ESSENTIAL IPRs in a timely fashion. In particular, a MEMBER submitting a technical proposal for a STANDARD or TECHNICAL SPECIFICATION shall, on a bona fide basis, draw the attention of ETSI to any of that MEMBER's IPR which might be ESSENTIAL if that proposal is adopted.

[4] *In re* Dell 121 F.T.C. 616, para 8.

FTC opined that Dell's non-disclosure would have caused harm to competition and affected consumer welfare".[5] Dell agreed not to enforce its patent pledged to the standard development and entered into a consent order.[6]

In *Rambus v Federal Trade Commission*,[7] Rambus participated in the standard development process of the Joint Electronic Device Engineering Council (JEDEC). During the development phase of dynamic random-access memory technology, Rambus failed to disclose information about the patent it owned, patent applications it had filed that were relevant to the standard development. FTC found that Rambus benefitted by participating in the standard development phase that enabled it to amend the pending patent applications. Rambus withdrew its membership from JEDEC and subsequently asked implementers of the DRAM standard to renegotiate the license as it had held patents that are relevant to the JEDEC standard. This resulted in FTC finding that Rambus violated the Sherman Act as it unlawfully monopolized the market through its deceptive conduct. However, the District Court of Columbia Circuit opined that the FTC failed to prove that lack of disclosure enabled Rambus to monopolize the market. It stated that:

> [A]n antitrust plaintiff must establish that the standard-setting organization would not have adopted the standard in question but for the misrepresentation or omission.

However, in Europe, the EC alleged that *Rambus* indulged in deceptive practices relating to patents that were relevant to DRAM standards developed by JEDEC. Non-disclosure of relevant patents to the SSO enabled Rambus to demand unreasonable royalties from implementers. Had Rambus disclosed the relevant patents at the time of the standard development process; SSO members would have the option of exploring alternatives that could have become part of the standard. EC was of the view that this amounted to abuse of dominant position and as such breached Article 102 of the TFEU. EC observed that standard setting process usually progresses based on declaration of the relevant proprietary rights owned or patent applications filed by the participants. This requires members to declare existing patents and pending patent applications on good faith basis as such declaration would enable SSO's to assess the availability of viable alternative technologies as well as secure a commitment from patent holders that they would license the technology on reasonable terms. JEDEC required members to disclose all patent related information as it relied on such compliance to assess and evaluate whether to include such technologies in the standard or to choose other viable alternatives. Rambus not only captured the standard by not providing patent-related information, but also locked the industry to a standard where members were not aware of patents owned by Rambus. EC opined that:

---

[5] Ibid.

[6] Ibid.

[7] *In the Matter of Rambus, Inc.*, No. 9302, at 4 (F.T.C. Aug. 2, 2006).

suppression of the relevant information necessarily distorted the decision-making process within a standard-setting body … save for Rambus' alleged deceit, JEDEC Members were likely to have designed a "patent-free" standard around Rambus' patents … there were substantial barriers to entry on the market and that the industry was locked into the JEDEC DRAM standards.[8]

EC emphasized that deceptive conduct does not in itself amount to abuse of dominance. However, the subsequent lock-in meant that implementers had to use the technologies owned by Rambus which was now in a position to assert that some of the relevant patents necessary to practice the standard is owned by it and is not subject to FRAND terms. This enabled Rambus to illegally monopolize the market as members would have to either pay the royalty demanded by Rambus or face infringement action or leave the market. EC closed the investigation as Rambus in its commitment proposed not to charge the JEDEC members for the past royalties and agreed to cap its royalties for the DRAM chips.

3.1 Non-disclosure Amounting to Equitable Doctrine of Implied Waiver

Standard setting organizations play a key role in developing new standards which enables interoperability of technologies among various competitors and as such facilitate wide dissemination of the underlying technologies. One of the key elements of participating in the standard setting process is that the patent holder submitting the patented technology agrees to offer licenses to all those seeking the license on a fair, reasonable, and non-discriminatory (FRAND) term. This commitment made toward the SSOs and third parties is the key foundation on the basis of which the standard setting process is undertaken. Any breach of the FRAND commitment by the patent holder after the adoption of standard would amount to deception as the breach of promise would enable the patent holder to exercise monopoly power as all prospective licensees would want to implement the standard and are forced to seek a license from the patent holder without having any recourse to alternative technology.

In *Qualcomm v Broadcom*, the key issue raised by Broadcom was that the breach of FRAND commitment by Qualcomm after the adoption of the patented Wideband Code Division Multiple Access (WCDMA) into the Universal Mobile Telecommunication Service (UMTS) standard amounted to anticompetitive behavior as it conferred monopoly power that enabled it to charge supra-competitive prices.[9] The Court of Appeals held that:

---

[8] Ibid.

[9] *Broadcom Corp. v. Qualcomm Inc.*, 501 F.3d 297 (3rd Cir. 2007).

(1) in a consensus-oriented private standard-setting environment, (2) a patent holder's intentionally false promise to license essential proprietary technology on FRAND terms, (3) coupled with an SDO's reliance on that promise when including the technology in a standard, and (4) the patent holder's subsequent breach of that promise, is actionable anticompetitive conduct.[10]

It further opined that a private standard setting environment requires all participants to fully disclose their underlying patented technology at the time of developing a standard and also agree to comply with the FRAND commitments. Non-observance of the FRAND commitment to prospective licensees also amounts to deception as it confers monopoly power on the patent holder. Such behavior results in "competitive harm" and denies prospective implementers who have adopted the standard no plausible alternative.[11]

4 Injunctive Relief

Injunctive relief is one of the rights enshrined in the Charter to Fundamental Rights.[12] In SEP-related matters SEP holders can use it effectively to compel implementers to enter into licensing agreement by threatening them with injunction suits. This may favor the SEP holders and thus distort competition.[13] On the other hand, refusal to grant injunctive relief to SEP holders in genuine cases might serve as an incentive to implementers not to enter into a licensing agreement or delay the negotiation process.[14] Therefore, it is necessary to have a framework to provide injunctive relief in disputes involving SEPs.

4.1 Pre-Huawei Jurisprudence

Depending on the facts of each case courts have dealt with interim injunction relief claims either in favor of SEP holder or in favor of implementer.[15] Lemley and Shapiro observed that:

---

[10] Ibid., at 313.

[11] Ibid.

[12] Charter of Fundamental Rights, art 47.

[13] Pierre Larouche and Nicolo Zingales, Injunctive Relief in the EU: Intellectual Property and Competition Law at the Remedies Stage *in* Jorge. L. Contreras (eds), *The Cambridge Handbook of Technical Standardization Law: Competition, Antitrust, and Patents* (Cambridge University Press, 2019).

[14] Ibid.

[15] Case Number AT.39939 *Samsung* - Enforcement of UMTS Standard Essential Patents (2014) Commission Decision OJ C350/8; *Motorola Mobility LLC and Google Inc.* (2013), FTC Docket No. C-4410 Decision and Order.

the threat of an injunction can enable a [SEP] holder to negotiate royalties far in excess of the patent holder's true economic contribution. Such royalty over-charges act as a tax on new products incorporating the patented technology, thereby impeding rather than promoting innovation.[16]

Therefore, courts across jurisdictions were reluctant provide to injunctive relief in cases involving SEPs as the patent holder is under an obligation to issue licenses on FRAND terms and the threat of injunctive relief would normally force an implementer to agree to royalty rates higher than FRAND terms.[17]

SSO policies further exacerbated the issue by excluding SEP holders from seeking injunctive relief. For instance, the IEEE policy ensured that the SEP holder was excluded from obtaining injunction against an unwilling licensee. The IEEE amendment on injunctive relief was phrased as:

A statement that the Submitter will make available a license for Essential Patent Claims to an unrestricted number of Applicants on a worldwide basis without compensation or under Reasonable Rates, with other reasonable terms and conditions that are demonstrably free of any unfair discrimination to make, have made, use, sell, offer to sell, or import any Compliant Implementation that practiced the Essential Patent Claims for use in conforming with the IEEE Standard. An Accepted LoA that contains such a statement signifies that reasonable terms and conditions, including without compensation or under Reasonable Rates, are sufficient compensation for a license to use those Essential Patent Claims and preclude seeking, or seeking to enforce, a Prohibitive Order except as provided in this policy. The Submitter of an Accepted LoA who has committed to make available a license for one or more Essential Patent Claims agrees that it shall neither seek nor seek to enforce a Prohibitive Order based on such Essential Patent Claim(s) in a jurisdiction unless the implementer fails to participate in, or to comply with the outcome of, an adjudication, including an affirming first-level appellate review, if sought by any party within applicable deadlines, in that jurisdiction by one or more courts that have the authority to: determine Reasonable Rates and other reasonable terms and conditions; adjudicate patent validity, enforceability, essentiality, and infringement; award monetary damages; and resolve any defenses and counterclaims. In jurisdictions where the failure to request a Prohibitive Order in a pleading waives the right to seek a Prohibitive Order at a later time, a Submitter may conditionally plead the right to seek a Prohibitive Order to preserve its right to do so later, if and when this policy's conditions for seeking, or seeking to enforce, a Prohibitive Order are met.[18]

The above amendment in the IEEE policy was contrary to universally acknowledged relief available to a patent holder when faced with the scenario of an unwilling

---

[16] Mark A. Lemley & Carl Shapiro, 'Patent Holdup and Royalty Stacking' (2006) 85 Tex. L. Rev. 1991, 1993.

[17] European Commission, 'Antitrust: Commission sends Statement of Objections to Motorola Mobility on potential misuse of mobile phone standard-essential patents' (Brussels, 6 May 2013) <http://europa.eu/rapid/press-release_IP-13-406_en.htm> accessed 29 April 2017; Alison Jones, 'Standard Essential Patents, FRAND Commitments Injunctions and the Smartphone Wars' (2014) 10(1) Eur. Comp. J. 1–36.

[18] IEEE-SA Standards Board Bylaws, s 6.1 (*IEEE* 2017) <http://standards.ieee.org/develop/pol icies/bylaws/sb_bylaws.pdf>.

licensee.[19] Injunctive relief is available to the SEP holder only in case the implementer does not abide by the arbitral award or decision of the court.[20] The other exceptions being instances wherein SEP holder could bring a claim against implementer were instances involving disputes related to reasonable rates of royalty, patent validity, essentiality, and award of monetary damages.[21] This had tilted the balance in favor of implementers, and SEP holders had very little leverage against infringers who were unwilling to seek license from SEP holder. Furthermore, it can also result in increased litigation between SEP holders.[22]

The Federal Circuit Court in *Apple, Inc. v Motorola Inc.*, stated that there was no such rule that per se prohibited the SEP holder from seeking injunctive relief in a FRAND encumbered SEP matter.[23] It stated that 'an injunction may be justified where an infringer unilaterally refuses a FRAND royalty or unreason—ably delays negotiations to the same effect'.[24] Moreover, the US Federal Trade Commission (USFTC), in *Google/Motorola* consent decree settlement, stated that injunctive relief should be available against unwilling licensees/infringers in certain limited situations.[25]

The revised IEEE policy, by making it conditional to seek injunctive relief, failed to provide a reasonable justification as to its qualified availability to SEP holders who have complied with the FRAND commitments.[26] This had often resulted in SEP holders failing to get injunctive relief in FRAND encumbered cases even though there had been a clear and blatant infringement of the said patents.[27] Courts had in the past refused to entertain claims for injunctive relief even in instances where there was nonpayment of royalties or patent hold-out or bad faith negotiation of licenses by implementers.[28] Theodore Essex, in his ITC Investigation report noted that:

---

[19] Micheal Frohlich, 'Report-Work Plan Item 5: Availability of Injunctive Relief for FRAND-Defense in Patent Infringement Proceedings' (*AIPPI*, March 2014) 5.

[20] Deepa Sundararaman, 'Inside the IEEE's Important Changes to Patent Policy' (*Law 360*, 3 April 2015).

[21] Ibid.

[22] Frohlich (n 19).

[23] Ibid. 9; *Apple, Inc. v Motorola, Inc.* (2014) Federal Circuit, Case No. 12-1548.

[24] Ibid. 1332.

[25] *Motorola Mobility L.L.C* (n 9).

[26] IEEE-SA Standards Board Bylaws, s 6.1 (IEEE, Draft No. 39 2014) (IEEE-SA Draft Standards) <http://grouper.ieee.org/groups/pp-dialog/drafts_comments/SBBylaws_100614_red-line_c urrent.pdf>.

[27] Daryl Lim, 'Standard Essential Patents, Trolls, and the Smartphone Wars: Triangulating the End Game' (2014) 119 Penn State Law Review 1.

[28] David Teece and Edward Sherry, 'The IEEE's New IPR Policy: Did the IEEE Shoot Itself in the Foot and Harm Innovation?' (2016) Tusher Center for the Management of Intellectual Capital Working Paper Series No. 13, 6. <http://businessinnovation.berkeley.edu/wp-content/uploads/2014/ 07/Tusher-Center-Working-Paper-No.-13.pdf>.

… standards implementers using the technology incorporated in the standard but without seeking a license or without engaging in licensing negotiations can lead to SEP holders filing a suit against and the standards implementers being forced to pay royalties at the FRAND rate, the same FRAND rate at which they were willing to pay the royalties in the first place.[29]

Such unwilling conduct on the part of implementers shifted the risks associated with negotiation of licenses and placed SEP holders at the mercy of implementers. Further, it would take away the incentive to participate in the standard setting process and pledge the underlying technology to become a standard if there was no prospect of earning royalties from implementers who could simply refuse to negotiate in good faith.[30] As Judge Essex succinctly summed up:

taking away the right to seek injunctive relief from SEP holders not only "puts the risk of loss entirely on the side of the patent holder," but also "encourages patent hold-out", which is as unsettling to a fair solution as any patent hold-up might be.[31]

Further, the Federal Court of Justice in Germany had developed the *Orange Book Standard*. In a patent infringement dispute, the defendant can set up a defense by stating that the conduct of the plaintiff amounted to an abuse of a dominant position which affects the fair competition in the market.[32] The defense can be raised by the defendant only if showed that it was ready to unconditionally accept the licensing terms at the royalty rate determined by the plaintiff and the defendant despite having reservations with the terms of the agreement pays the royalty through an escrow account.[33] The objective behind the standard is to prevent a patent holder from seeking injunction against the defendant who is willing to take a license. The standard relied more on the EU competition law to prevent a patent holder from seeking injunctive relief against the willing defendant who might have had disagreements as to what would be an appropriate royalty rate.[34] In SEP-related cases, the implementers who were willing to negotiate a license and paid in the escrow account would normally use this as a defense if the SEP holder sought injunctive relief against them.

---

[29] In re *Certain Wireless Devices with 3G and/or 4G Capabilities and Components Thereof* (2014) US International Trade Commission, Inv. No. 337-TA-868 113–14.

[30] Ibid. 114.

[31] Ibid.; Sandra Badin, 'Patent Hold-up or Patent Hold-out? Judge Essex adds his voice to the SEP-FRAND Debate' (*Intellectual Property Alert*, 10 July 2014) <https://www.mintz.com/newsletter/2014/Advisories/4096-0714-NAT-IP/4096-0714-NAT-IP.pdf>.

[32] Az. KZR 39/06.

[33] Ibid.

[34] Ibid.

4.2 Huawei v ZTE

In *Huawei Technologies Co. Ltd v ZTE*,[35] the Court of Justice in European Union (CJEU) stated that the following factors have to be met before an SEP holder can seek an injunctive relief:

> it is for the proprietor of the SEP to present to that alleged infringer a specific, written offer for a licence on FRAND terms, in accordance with the undertaking given to the standardisation body, specifying, in particular, the amount of the royalty and the way in which that royalty is to be calculated.

> ... where the proprietor of an SEP has given an undertaking to the standardisation body to grant licences on FRAND terms, it can be expected that it will make such an offer. Furthermore, ... the proprietor of the SEP is better placed to check whether its offer complies with the condition of non-discrimination than is the alleged infringer.

> ... it is for the alleged infringer diligently to respond to that offer, in accordance with recognised commercial practices in the field and in good faith, a point which must be established on the basis of objective factors, and which implies, in particular, that there are no delaying tactics.

> Should the alleged infringer not accept the offer made to it, it may rely on the abusive nature of an action for a prohibitory injunction or for the recall of products only if it has submitted to the proprietor of the SEP in question, promptly and in writing, a specific counteroffer that corresponds to FRAND terms.

> Furthermore, where the alleged infringer is using the teachings of the SEP before a licensing agreement has been concluded, it is for that alleged infringer, from the point at which its counteroffer is rejected, to provide appropriate security, in accordance with recognised commercial practices in the field, for example by providing a bank guarantee or by placing the amounts necessary on deposit. The calculation of that security must include, inter alia, the number of the past acts of use of the SEP, and the alleged infringer must be able to render an account in respect of those acts of use.

> In addition, where no agreement is reached on the details of the FRAND terms following the counteroffer by the alleged infringer, the parties may, by common agreement, request that the amount of the royalty be determined by an independent third party, by decision without delay.

> Lastly, ... an alleged infringer cannot be criticised either for challenging, in parallel to the negotiations relating to the grant of licences, the validity of those patents and/or the essential nature of those patents to the standard in which they are included and/or their actual use, or for reserving the right to do so in the future.[36]

In *Huawei*, the CJEU is focusing on the behavior of the implementer and the SEP holder.[37] It provided guidelines that an SEP holder has to follow in order to be eligible to file a suit against an implementer for patent infringement or even seek injunctive relief. These guidelines enable the SEP holder to avoid the pitfalls of violating Article 102 of TFEU.[38] In the process, the CJEU also requires the implementer to conduct itself in a manner that demonstrates its willingness to negotiate a

---

[35] Case C-170/13, *Huawei* Technologies v ZTE.

[36] *Huawei* (n 35), paras 62–69.

[37] Ibid.

[38] Ibid.

FRAND-encumbered license. If the implementer negotiates in good faith and follows the steps laid out by the CJEU, then it can claim abuse of dominance on the part of the SEP holder if the negotiation breaks down.[39] However, the CJEU failed to take into consideration that even if the SEP holder has notified the implementer there is a possibility wherein SEP holder could still be abusing its dominant position.[40]

The CJEU clearly laid down that seeking injunctions must not be seen as per se abusive practice on the part of the SEP holder. The factors laid down can further be split into multiple stages. The first step of issuing a written communication to the implementer about the existence of the SEPs and respective technological information should be treated as the *Notice Stage*. The SEP holder should first notify the implementer about the infringement. Notification should specify the patent numbers that have been infringed by the implementer along with information about the exact manner in which it has been infringed.[41] Subsequent stage wherein the SEP holder informs the implementer about the rate of royalty and the basis on which the royalty is calculated should be treated as an *Offer Stage*.[42] The SEP holder is required to make an offer to the implementer which should be on FRAND terms and also royalty that needs to be paid and the method of calculating the royalty. As stated by CJEU, the SEP holder who is encumbered by FRAND obligations needs to offer the license at a reasonable rate and has the obligation to ensure that the terms and conditions of the license are non-discriminatory. While making an offer, the SEP holder should ensure that it contains information related to undertaking given by it to the concerned SSO. For instance, the ETSI IPR Policy mandates that all SEP holders have to agree to give out FRAND encumbered license to all willing licensees.[43] Additionally, *Huawei* guidelines states that an offer should contain requisite information related to amount of royalty that needs to be paid and also specify the method of calculating royalty rates.[44] However, the judgment fails to specify the extent to which the detailed information needs to made in the offer.

As per the CJEU, the implementer is under an obligation to consider the offer made by SEP holder in good faith as per established commercial practices. If the implementer accepts the offer, it can be regarded as the *Acceptance or Response Stage*. This step is dependent upon the willingness demonstrated by the implementer to negotiate a FRAND-encumbered license with the SEP holder.[45] The implementer is expected to promptly respond to the offer made by the SEP holder in good faith. The implementer is expected to respond to offer keeping in mind the prevailing commercial practices and refrain from any delaying tactics (Response Stage).[46] The

---

[39] Ibid.

[40] Ibid., para 744.

[41] *Huawei* (n 35), para 61.

[42] Ibid., para 63.

[43] European Telecommunications Standards Institute, 'ETSI Intellectual Property Rights Policy' (2017) <http://www.etsi.org/images/files/ipr/etsi-ipr-policy.pdf> accessed 10 May 2018.

[44] *Huawei* (n 35), para 63.

[45] Ibid., para 63.

[46] Ibid., para 65.

Implementer can accept the offer, seek further clarification about the offer in the form of an enquiry, make a counteroffer, or reject the offer. It can be inferred from the *Huawei* guidelines the implementer needs to demonstrate diligence, respond to the offer as per the prevailing commercial practices, act in good faith, without delaying the negotiation of the license.[47] *Huawei* guidelines also notes that if the implementer rejects the offer made by the SEP holder, then it is necessary to make a counteroffer which is on FRAND terms in order insulate itself from any legal action that might be initiated by the SEP holder.[48]

In case there is disagreement as to the royalty rate or the terms of the license agreement, the implementer has the obligation to provide a counteroffer. This can be regarded as the *Counteroffer Stage*. If both parties are unable to agree upon the royalty rate, they have to reach out to an independent third party to decide the same without delay. The implementer can bring an action against the "abusive nature of the injunctive suit" filed by the SEP holder, but only after making a counteroffer which is on FRAND terms (Counteroffer stage).[49] If for any reason the negotiation could not be concluded between the parties, then the implementer is under an obligation to provide a security deposit as per commercial practice given that the implementer might be using the infringing patent.[50] An independent third party may be approached by the to parties determine the amount of royalty if the negotiation breaks down or if parties could not agree upon FRAND terms.[51]

As per CJEU, if an implementer is engaged in delaying the negotiation of license or acting in bad faith, then such conduct can be regarded as unwillingness on the part of the implementer and the SEP holder can seek injunctive relief as a remedy. Further, in a country like India, where IP awareness is still in its infancy and not pervasive, injunctive remedies can act as a deterrent against IP violations, create awareness about IP rights, and provide incentives for firms to invest in R&D, which is critical to make the 'Design in India' vision a reality. The CJEU has clearly ruled that if an implementer remains passive, unresponsive, or engages in delaying tactics after being approached to enter a licensing negotiation such implementer cannot be considered as 'willing'.[52] While the *Huawei* guidelines provided a general framework, there are many unanswered questions.

The *Huawei* ruling provides a framework to negotiate a license on FRAND terms and this requires the SEP holder to make an offer and the implementer to show willingness to negotiate a license. Unwillingness on the part of the implementer will allow the SEP holder to seek legal remedies for patent infringement, recover unpaid

---

[47] "… it is for the alleged infringer diligently to respond to that offer in accordance with recognized commercial practices in the field and in good faith, a point which must be established on the basis of objective factors and which implies, in particular, that there are no delaying tactics." Huawei (n 35), para 65.

[48] *Huawei* (n 35), para 66.

[49] *Huawei* (n 35), para 67.

[50] Ibid., para 67.

[51] Ibid., para 68.

[52] European Commission, 'Setting out the EU Approach to Standard Essential Patents' COM (2017) 712 final <https://ec.europa.eu/docsroom/documents/26583> accessed 10 January 2018.

royalties and claim damages. Despite the *Huawei* ruling, it must be noted that several cases have come up before the court wherein the primary contention is related to the reasonable period within which an implementer should respond to the offer. CJEU in *Huawei* deliberately left it unclear in order to enable the courts to decide reasonable time period based on the context of each case.

4.3 *Post* **Huawei**

The *Huawei* case came up before the CJEU as the court in Dusseldorf sought clarification regarding the approach courts are required to take in cases involving injunctive relief. Dusseldorf court wanted to understand whether it was required to apply the *Orange Book Standard*[53] or the jurisprudence developed in the *Samsung* and *Motorola* decisions.[54]

While negotiating license agreement it is fairly common for the parties to exchange multiple instances of offers, counteroffers, and clarifications about the terms of the agreement between the SEP holder and the implementer. The *Huawei* case does not clarify how this aspect needs to be treated. Would multiple exchanges between parties be regarded as negotiations done if good faith or will it be treated as delaying tactics? Some of these issues came up before the courts in EU countries.[55]

The *Huawei* guidelines have been applied by the German courts to determine the willingness of the parties to negotiate a license in good faith and determine whether parties have followed the negotiation process.[56]

The Regional Court in Dusseldorf has ruled that notice provided by the SEP holder serves as a possible instance wherein the implementer is notified of the requisite information related to the underlying SEPs and it could double up as notifying the implementer of possible subsequent legal action that could be taken by SEP holder if there is refusal to negotiate on the part of the implementer.[57] The CJEU decision in *Huawei* only lays down a general framework to negotiate a FRAND encumbered license between SEP holder and implementers. However, given that the CJEU only

---

[53] Case No. KZR 39/06O *Orange-Book-Standard* Bundesgerichtshof, Judgment dated 6 May 2009.

[54] *Samsung* (n); *Motorola* (n).

[55] Indranath Gupta, et al., 'Evolving *Huawei* framework: SEPs and Grant of Injunctions' in Ashish Bharadwaj, Vishwas H. Devaiah & Indranath Gupta (eds), *Multidimensional Approaches Towards New Technology* (Springer, 2018).

[56] Case No. 4a O 93/14 *Sisvel v Haier* (2015) LG Dusseldorf; Case No. 2 O 106/14 *Saint Lawrence v Deutsche Telekom* (2015) LG Mannheim; Case No. 4a O 74/14 *Saint Lawrence v Vodafone* (2016) LG Dusseldorf; Case No. 7 O 66/15 *NTT DoCoMo v HTC* (2016) LG Mannheim; Case No. 7 O 96/14 *Pioneer v Acer* (2016) LG Mannheim, Judgment dated 8 January 2016; Case No. 7 209/15 *Philips v Archos* (2016) LG Mannheim.

[57] Case No. 4a O 126/14 *Saint Lawrence v Vodafone* LG Dusseldorf, Judgment dated 31 March 2016, para 35.

laid down general norms without necessarily providing precise directions on certain aspects of the license negotiation, it has led to varied interpretations of the framework by the German courts.

4.3.1 Transitional Cases

The Huawei framework requires the SEP holder to notify the implementer that the SEP holders' specific patents have been infringed upon by the implementer and the notice needs to provide specific information about all the SEPs that have been used by the implementer and that they are required to take or negotiate a license with the SEP holder.[58] In *Pioneer v Acer*,[59] *Saint Lawrence v Vodafone*,[60] *Sisvel v Haier*,[61] the German courts granted SEP holders a 'transition time period' as all the cases were filed before the judgment in *Huawei*. As SEP holder was not required to formally notify the implementer about the instances of infringement before the decision in *Huawei* it was only fair that the above cases were treated as 'transitional cases'.[62] The notice of infringement served on the implementer by the SEP holder was considered as sufficient instance of providing notice in such 'transitional cases'. The German courts ruled that retrospective imposition of the notification requirement upon SEP holders would be unfair especially when the issue had progressed to subsequent stages of offer and counteroffer stage.[63] As the primary purpose or objective behind notifying the implementer was to equip them with all the necessary information about the SEPs, the German courts reasoned that the implementer had the necessary knowledge in all the above 'transitional cases' as the legal proceedings had already commenced.[64]

4.3.2 Willingness to Take a License

In *Pioneer v Acer*, the Dusseldorf Court noted that the *Huawei* case does not merely provide a framework to negotiate a license, rather it should be seen as a tool that can determine the willingness of the parties to negotiate a license in good faith.[65]

In *NTT DoCoMo*, the LG Mannheim Court and *Pioneer* reaffirmed that the SEP holder has an obligation to notify the implementer about the possible infringement

---

[58] *Huawei* (n 35), para 61.

[59] *Pioneer* (n 56), para 94.

[60] *Saint Lawrence* (n 56), para 232.

[61] Case No 4a O 144/14 *Sisvel v Haier* (2015) LG Dusseldorf, Judgment dated 3 November 2015, 29.

[62] *Pioneer* (n 56); *Saint Lawrence* (n 56); ibid.

[63] Jorge Contreras, *The Cambridge Handbook of Technical Standardization Law* (Cambridge University Press 2019) 427.

[64] Ibid. 427.

[65] *Pioneer* (n 56), para 87.

by the implementer and also specify the relevant patents that have been used by the implementer.[66] In *NTT DoCoMo*, the court observed that the notice sent to implementer must identify that the patents infringed by the implementer are part of a standard, identify the SEPs used by the implementer and the manner in which it has been used by the implementer.[67] The court noted that contents of the notice can vary and is dependent on the scenario of each case.[68] In *Saint Lawrence v Vodafone*, the Dusseldorf Court noted that the notice should clearly identify the patent by its publication number and the manner in which the said patent has been used by the implementer.[69] The Dusseldorf Court, in In *Saint Lawrence v Vodafone*, noted that notice must have been sent to the implementer before the SEP holder can make out any claim for injunctive relief in the court.[70]

Upon receiving the notice with relevant information about the specific patents that have been infringed, the implementer is required to respond and demonstrate willingness to negotiate a license with the SEP holder in good faith. In *Saint Lawrence v Deutsche Telekom, Sisvel v Haier* and *Saint Lawrence v Vodafone*, the German courts specifically observed the time taken by the implementer to respond to the notice received from the SEP holder.[71] In *Deutsche Telekom*, it was observed that a duration of more than three months taken by the implementer was too long and could be seen as an instance of unwillingness on the part of the implementer.[72] In *Saint Lawrence v Vodafone*, a delay of five months to respond to the notice was interpreted as too long a time taken by the implementer. Such delay can demonstrate the unwillingness on the part of the implementer to negotiate a license in good faith.[73] However, the Regional Court in *Saint Lawrence v Vodafone* noted that in order to determine unwillingness on the part of the implementer, it is necessary to take note of not only the duration taken to respond to the notice, but also the information provided by the SEP holder in the earlier notice.[74] For instance, the time taken to respond to a notice sent by the SEP holder would depend entirely on the kind of information provided in the notice. If the SEP holder has provided detailed information regarding the specific patents that have been infringed, then time taken to respond to such a notice should ideally be less. In case not enough information is available in the notice, it is only natural for the implementer to take more time to respond to such notice as the implementer would have to seek more clarification from the SEP holder.[75] In *Pioneer v Acer*, it was held that the implementer or its parent company's conduct

---

[66] *NTT DoCoMo* (n 56), para 57; *Pioneer* (n 56), para 74; *Huawei* (n 35), para 61.

[67] *NTT DoCoMo* (n 56), para 57.

[68] Ibid., para 57.

[69] *Saint Lawrence* (n 56), para 219.

[70] Ibid., para 223.

[71] *Deutsche Telekom* (n 56); Sisvel (n 56); Saint Lawrence (n 56).

[72] *Deutsche Telekom* (n 56).

[73] *Saint Lawrence* (n 56).

[74] Ibid., para 245.

[75] Ibid., para 252.

demonstrated unwillingness on its part to negotiate a license.[76] In *Sisvel v Haier*, it was held that willingness can only be determined based on the overall conduct of the implementer.[77]

If the implementer indicates his willingness to take a license on FRAND terms without imposing any condition, the SEP holder has the obligation to send an offer containing the relevant information related to the royalty and the basis on which its calculated.[78]

In *Tagivan (MPEG-LA) v Huawei*,[79] the implementers were negotiating a license with the MPEG LA's standard licensing agreement that was publicly available. Tagivan, the SEP holder, was part of the pool. However, the negotiation with the implementer failed despite several months of negotiation. Subsequently, the SEP holder sought for injunctive relief, rendering of accounts, destruction of infringing products and a declaration that the implementer is liable for infringement. While the matter was before the District Court of Dusseldorf, the implementer made counteroffers to the SEP holder limited to SEPs owned by them in the pool. The implementer went to the extent of even providing bank guarantee to the SEP holder. The Dusseldorf Court stated that if the SEP holder and implementer have followed the *Huawei* guidelines then there is no reason to worry even if the SEP holder has in a dominant position. It stated that both the parties must discharge their obligations in good faith by following the various steps indicated in the *Huawei* guidelines. It also affirmed that a notice of infringement sent to parent company essentially complies with the guidelines as long as the infringing patents have been identified and the specific instances of infringement are clearly mentioned in the notice. Further, it indicated that any response made by the parent company that received the notice will be treated as an indication of willingness to negotiate the license in good faith.

4.3.3 FRAND Terms

When an offer is made by the SEP holder, it is necessary to ensure that it is based on FRAND terms. The Regional Court of Dusseldorf noted that whether offer is on FRAND terms can be determined by looking at comparable license agreements entered by the SEP holder. If the terms of the licensing agreements are similar, then there is a likelihood that the royalty rate offered by the SEP holder is more likely to be on FRAND terms.[80] In order to determine whether different license agreements are on similar terms, it is necessary to compare them and understand the scope of the offer made by the SEP holder. In *Saint Lawrence v Vodafone*, the Regional Court stated that there is no single mathematical value or number that would meet the FRAND

---

[76] *Pioneer* (n 171).

[77] Case No. I-15 U 66/15, *Sisvel v Haier* OLG Dusseldorf, Judgment dated 13 January 2016.

[78] *Huawei* (n 35), para 63.

[79] Case No. 4a O 17/17, *Tagivan* (MPEG-LA) District Court (Landgericht) of Düsseldorf, Judgment dated 15 November 2018.

[80] *Saint Lawrence* (n 56), para 267.

requirement, rather a range of values that are 'fair, equitable and non-discriminatory' would be considered as FRAND.[81] It is absolutely necessary for the SEP holder to clearly specify the consideration for the FRAND-encumbered license agreement.[82] The SEP holder should have enough discretion to determine the FRAND terms.[83] If the offer made by the SEP holder is not accompanied with a comprehensible calculation of the royalties, then such an offer cannot be regarded as a FRAND offer.[84]

4.3.4   Obligation to Respond to the Offer

Willingness of the implementer to negotiate a license based on FRAND terms can be assessed based on the time take by the implementer to respond to such an offer.[85] The Regional Court of Mannheim in *Pioneer* opined that the implementer is under an obligation to respond to the offer made by SEP holder even though the implementer is of the opinion that such an offer is not on FRAND terms.[86] If the implementer has failed to respond to the offer made by SEP holder, the courts have been reluctant to examine whether the offer was made on FRAND terms as any delay or failure to respond to the offer is regarded as unwillingness on the part of the SEP holder.[87,88] In *Sisvel v Haier* the court determined unwillingness of the implementer based on the response provided by the implementer. In *Saint Lawrence v Deutsche Telekom*, it was held that while the implementer need not always agree with royalty rate offered by the SEP holder, the willingness on the part of the implementer can be determined based on the kind of counteroffer provided. If the counteroffer provided by the implementer is too restrictive, then it can be ruled by the court that there was unwilling conduct by the implementer. Therefore, a counteroffer that only restricts the license to one country or region would be treated as a restrictive counteroffer especially when the offer made by the SEP holder was for a worldwide license.[89] If there is no comprehensible method to calculate the royalty rate in the counteroffer, then it may not be considered as a 'concrete counteroffer'.[90] This is particularly the case as the implementer may be required to furnish a guarantee to the court during the negotiation process as there is no concrete reference point on the basis of which

---

[81] Ibid., para 314.

[82] Ibid., para 313.

[83] Case No. 6 U 58/16 2016, OLG Karlsruhe Resolution of 8 September 2016, para 36.

[84] *Philips* (n 56), para 112.

[85] *Huawei* (n 35), para 65.

[86] *Pioneer* (n 56), para 77.

[87] Ibid.; *Sisvel* (n 56).

[88] *Sisvel* (n 56) 30.

[89] *Deutsche* (n 56), para 59.

[90] Ibid., para 59.

royalty is determined by the implementer.[91] Further, any delay in making a written counter offer would mean that the implementer has failed to meet the obligation.[92]

4.3.5 Security Deposit

Negotiation of license is a continuous process and does not end when an offer is made by SEP holder or when a counteroffer is made by the implementer. There can be several instances of back-and-forth inquiry into the terms of the offer or counteroffer, and as such the entire process needs to be seen a continuous process. As per the *Huawei* guidelines, the SEP holder is under no obligation to accept the counteroffer and instead could reject the same. In such instances, the implementer should make a security deposit as per the acceptable commercial practices in order to demonstrate his willingness to negotiate and agree upon a FRAND-encumbered license.[93] Based on the *Huawei* guidelines, courts had multiple opportunities to emphasize on the need to deposit appropriate security with SEP holder within reasonable time frame as this would demonstrate that the implementer is willing to negotiate a license and also goes a long way in assuring the SEP holder is not denied of the adequate royalty while the negotiation is ongoing. In *Sisvel v Haier*, the court was of the opinion that the obligation of the implementer does not end with the making of a counteroffer. There can be instances wherein the SEP holder may not agree with the terms of the counteroffer, in such instances it is necessary for the implementer to assure the SEP holder that while the negotiation might go on for a while, it is prepared to make a security deposit for the continued use of the underlying SEP. Therefore, after the rejection of the counteroffer it is necessary for the implementer to render the accounts to SEP holder on a timely basis and provide a security deposit.[94] This demonstrates that the implementer is acting in good faith.[95] The obligation arises the moment the counteroffer is rejected by the SEP holder.[96] In the *Sisvel* case, the implementer took more than 12 months from the rejection of the counteroffer to deposit the security and render the accounts. The court deemed this as a delay on the part of the implementer. The court was of the opinion that the clock started ticking the moment the counteroffer was rejected by the SEP holder and timeframe to deposit security and render accounts should be interpreted in a narrow manner.[97] A delay of the kind noted in the *Sisvel case* would be seen as an instance of delaying tactic on the part of the implementer and could be interpreted as an unwilling conduct on the part of the implementer.[98] In *Pioneer*, the court opined that demonstration of

---

[91] Ibid., para 232.

[92] *NTT DoCoMo* (n 56), para 73.

[93] *Huawei* (n 35), para 67.

[94] *Sisvel* (n 56) 33.

[95] Ibid. 33.

[96] Ibid. 32.

[97] Ibid. 33.

[98] Ibid. 33.

willingness to negotiate a license in such instances would be based on the immediate steps taken by the implementer.[99] This would certainly involve immediate measures taken by the implementer to furnish security, as such a measure in the immediate aftermath of the rejection of the counteroffer would go a long way to demonstrate the willingness on the part of the implementer to negotiate a license.

4.3.6 *Unwired v Huawei*

Unwired Planet v Huawei dealt with the FRAND issue and competition concerns related to SEP licensing.[100] The Supreme Court of England was required to decide upon four specific issues which are as follows:

1. Is it appropriate for courts in England to exercise jurisdiction in SEP related cases where the parties have not agreed to it jurisdiction? Can the English courts exercise the power to grant injunctions against the implementer and decide upon royalty rate?
2. Whether the English courts should have stayed the proceedings citing *forum non conveniens*?
3. Whether English courts can issue global FRAND rates and how does one go about the non-discrimination prong of the FRAND requirement?
4. Whether all aspects of the *Huawei* guidelines have to be followed for the SEP holder to file for injunctive relief and whether noncompliance of any aspect of the guidelines would enable the implementer to claim abuse of dominance against the SEP holder.

While ruling on the first issue, the Supreme Court observed that:

> We agree with the parties that the FRAND obligation in the IPR Policy he IPR Policy is intended to have international effect, as its context makes clear. This is underlined by the fact that the undertaking required of the owner of an alleged SEP extends not only to the family of patents (subject only to reservations entered pursuant to clause 6.2 of the IPR Policy) but also to associated undertakings, as stated in the declaration forms in the IPR Policy. In imposing those requirements and more generally in its requirement that the SEP owner makes an irrevocable undertaking to license its technology, ETSI appears to be attempting to mirror commercial practice in the telecommunications industry. We do not accept the distinction which Huawei draws (in its third submission above (para 53)) between voluntary agreements which operators in the telecommunications industry choose to enter into on the one hand and the limited powers of a court on the other, since the IPR Policy envisages that courts may determine whether or not the terms of an offered licence are FRAND when they are asked to rule upon the contractual obligation of a SEP owner which has made the irrevocable undertaking required under the IPR Policy. It is to be expected that commercial practice in the relevant market is likely to be highly relevant to an assessment of what terms are fair and reasonable for these purposes. Moreover, the IPR Policy envisages that the parties

---

[99] *Pioneer* (n 56), para 87.
[100] *Unwired Planet v Huawei*, [2020] UKSC 37.

will first seek to agree FRAND terms for themselves, without any need to go to court; and established commercial practice in the market is an obvious practical yardstick which they can use in their negotiation. In our view the courts below were correct to infer that in framing its IPR Policy ETSI intended that parties and courts should look to and draw on commercial practice in the real world.[101]

The Supreme Court opined that there is no harm in a national court setting the global FRAND rates and exercise its jurisdiction and to this effect it pointed out to several SEP-related cases decided by courts in other jurisdictions that indicated the willingness to exercise jurisdiction. The Supreme Court noted that if a case involves patents that were granted in UK, it is a good enough ground to intervene. It noted that "in the context of a global standard it is disproportionate to exclude an implementer from the UK market unless it enters into a worldwide licence of untested patents solely because it has infringed a UK patent".[102] If the issue involves national patents, then the English courts have every right to determine the validity of such patents and also determine the infringement of such patents. It examined ETSI's IPR policy and held that the policy enables the SEP holder to seek an injunctive relief and also enabled courts to decide upon a global license. It held that it's only fair for the English courts to determine whether an injunction is to be granted and also decide upon appropriate remedy when the issue involves a UK patent being infringed upon.[103]

Huawei had raised the issue whether the English court were the appropriate forum given that Chinese companies were involved in the case and China might have been the appropriate forum to decide the case. To this, UK Supreme Court stated the parties had not showed that China was the appropriate forum as an alternative to the courts in England and Wales. The UK Supreme Court opined that:

> the English court does have such a jurisdiction, even in the absence of consent by the parties, and it has of course exercised that jurisdiction in the Unwired case. Directions have been given in the Conversant case (subject to the outcome of this appeal) for it to be done again. Furthermore, against the speculative possibility that the Chinese courts might accept jurisdiction to settle a global FRAND licence by consent, there is the judge's finding that Conversant had acted reasonably in refusing to give its consent, for reasons connected with the conditions which the appellants sought to impose, a conclusion which was not met with any persuasive challenge in this court.[104]

The Supreme Court opined that there is an obligation on the part of the SEP holder to seek a global license, and this is enough reason for the English courts to intervene.[105]

While deciding on how to go about determining the non-discrimination prong of the FRAND terms, the court stated that:

> that the non-discrimination element in the FRAND undertaking is "general" and not "hard-edged" and that there had been no breach of it. The "non-discriminatory" part of the relevant

---

[101] Unwired (n 100), para 62.

[102] Ibid., para 86.

[103] Ibid.

[104] Ibid.

[105] Ibid., para 98.

phrase gives colour to the whole and provides significant guidance as to its meaning. It provides focus and narrows down the scope for argument about what might count as "fair" or "reasonable" for these purposes in a given context. It indicates that the terms and conditions on offer should be such as are generally available as a fair market price for any market participant, to reflect the true value of the SEPs to which the licence relates and without adjustment depending on the individual characteristics of a particular market participant. Put another way, there is to be a single royalty price list available to all ... [s]ince price discrimination is the norm as a matter of licensing practice and may promote objectives which the ETSI regime is intended to promote (such as innovation and consumer welfare), it would have required far clearer language in the ETSI FRAND undertaking to indicate an intention to impose the more strict, "hard-edged" non-discrimination obligation for which Huawei contends.[106]

The court opined that while reading the term FRAND, it should be understood as a composite whole and should not be interpreted to have two different obligations. This meant that there is no need to interpret FRAND as having a fair and reasonable obligation as one prong and separately requiring the non-discriminatory prong.[107] The Supreme Court was required to decide whether the Huawei guidelines required the SEP holder to make FRAND offer, failing which he cannot seek injunctive relief. It was required to decide whether the FRAND offer made by the SEP holder acted as a safe harbor that prevented a finding of anticompetitive behavior. The Supreme Court noted that:

it is for the proprietor of the SEP to present to that alleged infringer a specific, written offer for a licence on FRAND terms, in accordance with the undertaking given to the standardisation body, specifying, in particular, the amount of the royalty and the way in which that royalty is to be calculated.

Then, it is for the alleged infringer "diligently to respond to that offer, in accordance with recognised commercial practices in the field and in good faith", with "no delaying tactics", and "it may rely on the abusive nature of an action for a prohibitory injunction ... only if it has submitted ... promptly and in writing, a specific counter-offer that corresponds to FRAND terms".

Thus, it was necessary for the SEP holder to notify the implementer of the infringement and upon an expression of willingness make FRAND-encumbered offer, and it is necessary for the implementer to respond without any delay, and in case a counter offer is made, it is necessary to make a security deposit for the continuing use of the infringing while continuing to negotiate the agreement in good faith. If the SEP holder brings an action for injunctive relief without notifying the implementer of the infringement, then it amounts to a possible infringement of the Article 102 of the TFEU.

---

[106] Ibid., paras 112, 114 and 124.

[107] Ibid., para 113.

4.3.7 Non-disclosure Agreements

It is often necessary for the SEP holder to insist that the implementer should sign a non-disclosure agreement (NDA) as relevant technological information and know-how is disclosed to the implementer during the process of license negotiation. Implementer might refuse to sign the NDA resulting the collapse of the license negotiations or at times delaying the process.

In *OLG Dusseldorf* case,[108] the SEP holder was trying to conclude a portfolio licensing agreement with two implementers while suit for damages were continuing in the courts. The implementers though refused to sign the NDA during the pendency of the proceedings as they alleged that the SEP holder intend to protect the industrial secrets. The implementers on the other hand brought proceedings against the SEP holder stating that the insistence on signing the NDA was not in accordance with the FRAND obligations of the SEP holder. This resulted in a countersuit for injunctive relief brought by the SEP holder. While deciding both the suits, the court opined that the implementers' refusal to sign the NDA does not absolve the SEP holder from carrying out his obligations as per the *Huawei* guidelines. However, the court noted if the implementers refuse to sign the agreement without any justification, then it might reduce the burden placed on the SEP holder to provide an explanation for the conditions laid out in the licensing agreement.

The Higher District Court of Dusseldorf in a case involving SEPs stated that it is necessary to examine whether the SEP holders claim related to confidential information is necessary and needs protection.[109] If the response to that inquiry is in the affirmative, then it might be necessary to protect such confidential information and only limited access may be provided to the implementer. However the SEP holder who is insisting on the confidentiality of business information is required to provide justification as to why such business information needs to be treated as confidential and also specify the measures that is necessary to protect such information. The SEP holder needs to clearly demonstrate how it would be inconvenienced if such business information is disclosed to third parties. The SEP holder who is giving out a FRAND encumbered license is under an obligation to be transparent towards all the stakeholders and if any information has to be kept confidential it is necessary to provide a justification to the implementer.

5 Developments in India

In India there have been several instances wherein the implementers have refused to sign the license agreement on the pretext that the terms are onerous, or the seat of arbitration is in a different jurisdiction, or that it requires them to sign NDA agreements or on the basis that the royalty rate is very high. In several instances

---

[108] *OLG Dusseldorf*, (*18* July 2017) Case No. I-2 U 23/17.

[109] *OLG Dusseldorf*, (25 April 2018) Case No. I-2 W 8/18, Higher District Court of Düsseldorf.

the refusal to negotiate or sign the agreement had exceeded more than three or four years resulting in the SEP holder seeking injunctive relief in the Delhi High Court. In some instances, implementers brought in parallel proceedings by filing complaints before the Competition Commission of India (CCI) alleging abuse of dominance by SEP holders. The CCI in such cases accommodated the complaints filed by infringing implementers who had failed to negotiate the license on FRAND terms. This unfortunate scenario has exposed the SEP holder to multiple proceedings. Refusal to negotiate the license or delaying tactics by the implementers have forced the SEP holders to seek injunctive relief, while any such approach for injunctive relief by SEP holders enabled the implementers to file complaints before the CCI.[110]

While deciding on injunctive relief, the Delhi High Court has followed slightly different approaches in Micromax and Intex case. In the Micromax case the Delhi High Court restricted the implementer from importing infringing product and in the Intex case, the court restricted the implementer from stelling or promoting of product incorporating the infringing SEPs.[111] It must be noted that in both the cases, the implementers engaged in bad faith negotiation of the license, refused to take the license, continued to use the underlying SEPs without making any deposit to the SEP holder, delayed the entire process of negotiation, and also brought parallel proceedings against the SEP holder. Despite this, the Delhi High Court did not declare them as unwilling licensees.

The implementers have demonstrated their unwillingness to negotiate the license at multiple levels. There have been instances wherein the implementers have been totally unresponsive when the SEP holder sent them a notice of infringement specifying the instances of infringement. Further, implementers have demonstrated their unwillingness by raising several issues that are not directly pertinent to the license agreement. These issues have been raised after an offer has been made by the SEP holder. SEP license negotiations have happened over several years. In cases involving Ericsson trying to negotiate a license with implementers like Intex, Lava, and iBall, negotiations were delayed and carried out over a period of five, four, and three years, respectively.[112] The Delhi High Court in these instances thought the implementers

---

[110] Avirup Bose, 'Emerging FRAND Jurisprudence of India - to License or not to License' *The Economic Times* (8 December 2015).

[111] *Telefonaktiebolaget LM Ericsson (Publ) v Mercury Electronics & Anr*, CS (OS) No. 442 of 2013, CS (COMM) 155/2017, Delhi High Court (*Ericsson v Micromax*).

[112] Negotiation went on for more than 5 years, Telefonaktiebolaget LM Ericsson (Publ) v Intex Technologies (India) Limited, CS (OS) No. 1045/2014 CS (COMM) 769 of 2016, Delhi High Court (*Ericsson v Intex*); Ericsson negotiated for nearly 4 years with Lava when Ericsson discovered that Lava had filed for declaration before the District Judge of Gautam Budhnagar, *Ericsson v Lava* (2015) Delhi High Court, Case No. CS (OS) 764 of 2015, paras 48, 53; Ericsson notified iBall regarding the infringement of its patent and also expressed its willingness to negotiate a license on FRAND terms, *iBall* (n 112), para 15. The negotiations went on for 4 years, Telefonaktiebolaget LM Ericsson (Publ) v iBall Technologies CS (OS) No CS (OS) 2501/2015 (COMM) 2501 of 2015, Delhi High Court (*Ericsson v iBall*), para 11.

were 'unwilling' to negotiate a license.[113] Taking these above cases into consideration it can be summed up that there were two stages of negotiations, the offer stage and the counter offer stage, which took too long due to the concerns over the Non-Disclosure Agreement.[114]

The Delhi High Court did not declare unwillingness on the part of the implementer based on their conduct during the offer stage or the counter-offer stage, rather it determined unwillingness based on the overall conduct of the implementer and the time taken by them to negotiate the royalty rate after the initial offer was made by the SEP holder.[115,116] The Delhi High Court observed that the negotiations were done in bad faith and there was a visible unwilling conduct on the part of the implementers.[117]

It is also necessary to understand that the reason for extended periods of negotiations between implementers and the SEP holder is primarily due to the lack of awareness on the part of the implementers about the complex nature of SEP license agreements. This resulted in reluctance on the part of the implementers to understand what constitutes fair, reasonable, and non-discriminatory terms of agreement.[118]

6 Antisuit Injunction

SEP litigation has become more complex in recent years as parties to the litigation are increasingly moving from one jurisdiction to another to counter the other party from gaining an upper hand. The objective behind suing in multiple jurisdictions is to primarily force the other party to enter into a settlement without the court actually passing a verdict in the matter. Apple and Qualcomm,[119] Motorola and

---

[113] The court ruled that: "… defendant … is also unwilling to execute a FRAND license", *Intex* (n 112), para 147. In the *iBall* case it stated that: "the defendant has prima facie acted in bad faith during the negotiations with plaintiff, it has even approached various fora and has made contrary statements in order to get monetary benefit", *Intex* (n 112), para 148.

[114] "[Intex] refused to enter into an NDA despite which the plaintiff held various meetings with the defendant to discuss its FRAND licensing program. But despite meeting, the defendant did not enter into the NDA", *Intex* (n 43), para 23.

[115] *iBall* (n 112), para 79.

[116] *Intex* (n 112), para 148; *iBall* (n 112), paras 26–27.

[117] Ibid.

[118] [iBall] stated that "it is merely a vendor and imports all its telecommunication devices from China and as such is not aware about any such infringement and if there is an infringement, it is only 'an innocent infringer'", *iBall* (n 112), para 15.

[119] *Apple v Qualcomm*, 2017 WL3966944 (SD Cal 2017).

Microsoft,[120] Samsung and Ericsson,[121] Samsung and Huawei,[122] Nokia and Intercontinental, Xiaomi[123] and InterDigital are some of the instances wherein the SEP litigation started in one continent and very quickly moved to multiple jurisdictions in other continents.

Antisuit injunction is largely a mechanism wherein an effort is made by one of the parties to an SEP litigation to move the court in a particular jurisdiction to restrain the other party in the SEP litigation to seek or continue proceedings in a foreign jurisdiction. While this sort of a move from a party enables it to consolidate all its disputes in a related set of issues to a single jurisdiction, it can trigger an Anti-anti suit injunction (AASI) by the other party in a forum of its choice trying to prevent the enforcement of the ASI.[124]

Microsoft brought an action against Motorola in the US as it had failed to offer a license on FRAND terms.[125] Motorola then brought an infringement action against Microsoft in Germany which had an impact on Microsoft's sale of software products.[126] Microsoft then sought an ASI against Motorola in the US so that Motorola could be prevented from enforcing the German Court order against Microsoft. The court in US granted an ASI and also called into question the timing of the infringement suit brought up before the court in Germany when the issue was pending in the US.[127]

Similarly, Huawei brought an infringement action against Samsung in the US as parties were unable to enter into a licensing agreement since the last 5 years.[128] Huawei also filed a suit against Samsung in China and the matter was decided very quickly in the Shenzhen Court which held that Samsung had infringed two patents owned by Huawei. Subsequently, Samsung sought for an ASI against Huawei in the US courts in order to prevent Huawei from enforcing the order of the Shenzhen court.

Ericsson had filed a suit in the US courts against Samsung alleging that it had failed to comply with the FRAND terms while renewing a global licensing agreement.[129] Samsung had filed a suit before the Wuhan Court seeking a declaratory judgment that the licensing terms are as per FRAND terms and also sought for a world wide ASI against Ericsson.[130] The purpose of the ASI was to prevent Ericsson from litigating

---

[120] *Microsoft Corp v Motorola* Inc., 696 F.3d 872 (9th Cir. 2012).

[121] *Ericsson v Samsung* WL 89980 (ED Tex 2021).

[122] *Huawei v Samsung*, WL 1784056 (ND Cal 2018).

[123] *Interdigital v Xiaomi*, A. 8772/2020 in CS (COMM) 295/2020.

[124] Maximilian Haedicke, Anti-Suit Injunctions, FRAND Policies and the Conflict between Overlapping Jurisdictions, (2022) 71 (2) *GRUR International* 101–112.

[125] *Microsoft Corp v Motorola* Inc., 696 F.3d 872 (9th Cir. 2012).

[126] Giuseppe Colangelo and Valerio Torti, Anti-suit Injunctions and Geopolitics in Transnational SEPs Litigation (December 3, 2021). Working Paper.

[127] Microsoft Corp v Motorola Inc, 696 F.3d 872 (9th Circuit 2012).

[128] *Huawei v Samsung*, Case No 3:16-cv-02787 (N.D. California 2018).

[129] *Ericsson v Samsung* WL 89980 (ED Tex 2021).

[130] Wuhan Intermediate People's Court, Case, E 01 Zhi Min Chu No 743 (2020), *Samsung v Ericsson*.

the FRAND matter in any other jurisdiction. Wuhan court granted a wide ASI against Ericsson which triggered an AASI being sought against Samsung in the US court. While granting the AASI, the US court noted that the effect of the wide ASI was to primarily frustrate Ericsson from seeking statutory relief that was available to Ericsson.

Xiaomi and Interdigital were involved in a multijurisdictional litigation involving SEPs. Xiaomi sought for a declaration in Wuhan that Interdigital's licensing terms were not in compliance with FRAND and Interdigital brought an infringement action and sought injunctive relief against Xiaomi in the Delhi High Court. Xiaomi then filed for an ASI against Interdigital in Wuhan to prevent them from litigating the matter in other jurisdictions while litigation was pending before the Wuhan Court.[131] The ASI granted by the Wuhan court was very wide which asked Interdigital to refrain from seeking injunctive relief in any court. Interdigital sought an ASI against Xiaomi in Germany and the Delhi High Court. The ASI was granted to Interdigital, and it prevented Xiaomi from enforcing the decision of the Wuhan court. Thus, it can be summed up that seeking ASI and AASI have become common among SEP holders and implementers, and this has resulted in multiple suits being filed in multiple jurisdictions without necessarily resulting in any decisive outcome or enforcement of the dispute between the parties.

7 Conclusion

SEP licensing negotiations can be complex and result in disagreements between the parties. Lack of clarity to negotiate a FRAND-encumbered license had resulted in multiple cases across the globe resulting in uncertainty as to what conditions have to be fulfilled to negotiate a license on FRAND terms. Lack of guidelines to negotiate a successful license meant that the SEP holder and implementers were wasting precious resources in fighting litigations. The Huawei framework enabled the parties to negotiate the license by following the various steps or stages. However, the CJEU deliberately laid out broad guidelines enabling the parties to negotiate the license as per global commercial or business practices. However, this in itself resulted in multiple suits before the courts to determine the willingness of the parties to negotiate the license in good faith. Further, the *Unwired* case elaborated on how FRAND needs to be interpreted and clarified that parties are negotiating a global FRAND license. However, despite some major developments that have clarified how parties can negotiate a FRAND license, we have witnessed an increase in SEP related litigation wherein parties are suing in multiple jurisdictions and indulging in forum shopping.

---

[131] Wuhan Intermediate People's Court, Case E 01 Zhi Min Chu No 169 (2020); *Xiaomi Communication Technology v Inter Digital Inc*; *Interdigital v Xiaomi*, A. 8772/2020 in CS (COMM) 295/2020.

Annexure I: Membership Application Form for TSDSI

Telecommunications Standards Development Society, India

Membership Application / Renewal form for Financial Year 2020–21

☐ New Membership of TSDSI   ☐ Renewal of Membership of TSDSI

To,
The Director General,
Telecommunications Standards Development Society, India (TSDSI)
Regd. Office: 2nd Floor, C-DOT Campus, Mandi Road, Mehrauli, New Delhi 110030

1	Name of the organization	
2	Type of the organization (Select only one type)	☐ Private ☐ Government ☐ PSU ☐ Statutory ☐ Startup / SME ☐ Autonomous ☐ Foreign
3	Address: a) Registered: b) Correspondence:	
4	Organisation profile (Brief Summary of the Organization from ICT/Telecom Standards perspective) (Please attach additional sheet if required)	
5	Designated contact person (Name, Mobile, phone, fax, email and whatsapp no)	

(continued)

© The Editor(s) (if applicable) and The Author(s) 2022
V. H. Bharadwaj et al., *Locating Legal Certainty in Patent Licensing*,
https://doi.org/10.1007/978-981-15-0181-4

(continued)

6	Email ID of the additional representatives to be Added in the TSDSI email groups (Tick the box where need to add) (Mandatory for new members, please attach additional sheet if required)	☐ SGN: ☐ SGSS: ☐ All_Members:
7	Organization Website URL	
8	ICT Verticals/Entity (Please select only one in the list as per applicant's main line of business)	1) Telecom Network Equipment Manufacturers with Indian product related IPR / Licensed Indian design or technology ☐ 2) Domestic Telecom Network Equipment Manufacturers ☐ 3) Telecom Service Providers ☐ 4) Any Other Service Providers like Service providers under UL (other than those in Sl no 3 above)/ISP/VNO/ Cloud Service Providers, Broadcasters, etc. ☐ 5) Applications/ Solutions Developers/Application Software / Service Platform Developers/ Digital communication Software Developers or providers of services mentioned here (but not covered in 3 and 4 above) ☐ 6) Semiconductor components designer/manufacturer ☐ 7) Terminal Equipment Manufacturers: Manufacturers of Mobile Device / CPE/ End User Devices ☐ 8) R&D organisation ☐ 9) Academic Institutions ☐ 10) Government Department/ Statutory or Autonomous bodies/organizations set up by the Government or Statutory or autonomous bodies ☐ 11) Any other entity in ICT enabled product manufacturing/ service/ solution provider domain (not covered elsewhere) ☐ 12) Associate Member: A) Indian Entity ☐ B) Foreign Entity ☐ (*Please refer 'Annexure B' at the end of document to check the general requirements and documents needed for eligibility for each vertical)
9	Turnover as per last audited balance Sheet	
10	GST No.	

(continued)

(continued)

11	**Please list areas of your interest and Intended areas of contribution in TSDSI (Please attach additional sheet if required)**	
12	**How did you come to know about TSDSI**	

Declarations:

1. I have been authorized by my organization to sign this document and have the legal authority to bind the applicant Administration/Organisation to the representations and commitments provided in this application form. (Please attach a copy of authorization by the competent authority like board resolution, General Power of Attorney etc.)
2. My organisation agrees to abide by the followings:

Extant Rules and Regulations of TSDSI □

IPR policy of TSDSI □

All the decisions taken by the General Body of TSDSI □

<Signed> Name: Designation: Name of the organization: Address: e-mail Address: Date:	**Seal of the organization**

To be filled by TSDSI Secretariat on receipt of complete documentation

Membership Fee Category (Please refer Annexure A)	Corporate Category 1 Fee Category A □ B □ C □ D □ E □ Category 2 □ Category 3 □ Category 4 □	
Checked By:	**Name:**	**Signature:**
Authorized By:	**Name:**	**Signature:**

Annexure A <u>Fee Applicable for Financial Year 2020–21:</u>

Membership Fee Category	Fee Category	Admission Fee (INR)	Annual Subscription Fee (INR)
Corporate	1		
I) INR 10 Crore > Annual Turnover <= INR 100 Crore	1A	2,00,000	2,67,500
II) INR 100 Crore > Annual Turnover <= INR 1000 Crore	1B	2,00,000	4,28,000
III) Annual Turnover > Rs. 1000 Crore	1C	2,00,000	8,82,750
IV) R&D organizations	1D	2,00,000	2,67,500
V) Annual Turnover <= INR 10 Crore	1E	1,00,000	1,33,750
VI) Academic Institutions, Not-for-Profit R&D organizations Government Department/ Statutory or Autonomous bodies/organizations set up by the Government or Statutory or autonomous bodies	2	1,00,000	1,33,750
Associate (Indian Entities)	3	1,00,000	1,33,750
Associate (Foreign Entities)	4	USD 1,600	USD 2,675

NOTE

i) *18% GST is applicable on all the membership categories.*
ii) *Fee applicable for any organization mentioned in serial no. 8 above in application form*

Annexure B <u>ICT VERTICAL CATEGORY</u>

S.N.	Type of vertical	Minimum Qualifying Criteria	Documents Required
1	Telecom Network Equipment Manufacturers with Indian product related IPR / Licensed Indian design or technology	1. The applicant Company should be registered and headquartered in India 2. The applicant should have ownership of substantial IPR related to a telecom Product or should be a manufacturer of a telecom Product using substantial IPR licensed from an Indian owner of the design/technology/IPR. 3. Manufacturing of a telecom product should be one of the objectives listed in the MoA (or a legally equivalent document) of the applicant company. 4. Manufacturing of the product should be undertaken through applicant's own facility in India or through contract manufacturing in India.	1. Copies of Registration, PAN and GST Certificate 2. As a proof of turnover Balance Sheet or relevant pages from annual report indicating the turnover of the applicant company duly certified by a director or company secretary. 3. Name of the product being manufactured and copy of MoA of the applicant company highlighting manufacturing as an objective. 4. Self-declaration satisfying following criteria: i. More than 50% of technology patents filed/granted shall be owned by the applicant company. ii. The Patents mentioned in 4 (i) above can be priority filed in India or abroad. Details of Patents numbers (filed/granted) to be provided. iii. Telecom Equipment is manufactured by the applicant company in a plant in India (details of plant location and its registration to be provided). 5. If manufacturing outsourced: i. Copy of certificate of registration in India of the company owning the plant and manufacturing the product of the applicant company. ii. Copy of Registration of the plant in India. iii. Invoice copy raised from the company owning plant to the applicant company (Financial figures can be masked). 6. In case the manufactured product is licensed from an Indian Design or Technology Organisation, the following documents apart from those mentioned in 1, 2 and 3 and 4(iii) above shall be submitted. i. Name of the Design/Technology Owner entity. ii. Copy of license agreement (financials may be masked if so desired by the applicant company. iii. A certificate from the authorized signatory of designer/technology owner company that the design/technology is owned by that company. iv. Documents listed at 4(i) and 4(ii) to be submitted by the Design /technology owner company

(continued)

(continued)

S.N.	Type of vertical	Minimum Qualifying Criteria	Documents Required
2	Domestic Telecom Network Equipment Manufacturers	1. The applicant Company should be registered in India	1. Copies of Registration, PAN and GST Certificate
		2. Manufacturing of a telecom product should be one of the objectives listed in the MoA (or a legally equivalent document) of the applicant company	2. As a proof of turnover Balance Sheet or relevant pages from annual report indicating the turnover of the applicant company duly certified by a director or company secretary.
		3. Manufacturing of telecom products should be undertaken through applicant's own facility in India or through contract manufacturing in India.	3. Name of the product being manufactured and copy of MoA of the applicant company highlighting manufacturing as an objective.
			4. Self-declaration that the Telecom Equipment is manufactured by the applicant company in a plant in India (Details of Plant location and its registration to be provided).
			5. If manufacturing is outsourced:
			i. Copy of certificate of registration of the company owning the plant and manufacturing the product of the applicant company.
			ii. Copy of Registration of the plant.
			iii. Invoice copy raised from the company owning plant to the applicant company (Financial figures can be masked).
3	Telecom Service Providers	1. The applicant Company should be registered in India	1. Copies of Registration, PAN and GST Certificate
		2. The telecom services should be one of the objectives listed in the MoA (or a legally equivalent document) of the applicant company.	2. As a proof of turnover Balance Sheet or relevant pages from annual report indicating the turnover of the applicant company duly certified by a director or company secretary.
		3. The Company should be holding a valid license from the Department of Telecommunications to provide one or more telecom services namely Access, NLD, ILD under Unified License (UL) or Unified Access Service License (UAS) except for those mentioned in Sl. No. 4	3. Copy of MoA of the applicant company highlighting provision of telecom services as an objective.
			4. Certified copy of valid UAS/UL/other license, as listed in column 3(3), from DoT.

(continued)

(continued)

S.N.	Type of vertical	Minimum Qualifying Criteria	Documents Required
4	Any Other Service Providers like Service providers under UL other than those in Sl no 3 above/ISP/VNO/ Cloud Service Providers, Broadcasters, etc	1. The applicant Company should be registered in India 2. The telecom services should be one of the objectives listed in the MoA (or a legally equivalent document) of the applicant company. 3. The applicant Company should be holding one or more valid license from Department of Telecommunications to provide Services under UL other than those in Sl no 3 above/ISP/VNO services/Cloud services or any other services based on valid license/registration/empanelment for Digital Communications from the Government in India.	1. Copies of Registration, PAN and GST Certificate 2. As a proof of turnover Balance Sheet or relevant pages from annual report indicating the turnover of the applicant company duly certified by a director or company secretary. 3. Copy of MoA of the applicant company highlighting provision of one or more services as mentioned in 4(3) as an objective. 4. Copy of valid license/registration/ empanelment from the relevant Government authority as applicable for one or more services mentioned in 4(3).
5	Applications/ Solutions Developers/ Application Software / Service Platform Developers/ Digital communication Software Developers or providers of services mentioned here (but not covered in 3 & 4 above)	1. The applicant Company should be registered in India 2. Applications/ Solutions Development/ Application Software / Service Platform Development/ Digital communication Software Development should be one of the objectives listed in the MoA (or a legally equivalent document) of the applicant company. 3. The applicant company should be in the business of development of Application Solutions, Platforms /Application Software / Service Platform / Digital communication Software providing services in these areas in India.	1. Copies of Registration, PAN and GST Certificate 2. As a proof of turnover Balance Sheet or relevant pages from annual report indicating the turnover of the applicant company duly certified by a director or company secretary. 3. Copy of MoA of the applicant company highlighting provision of one or more services as mentioned in 5(3) as an objective. 4. Copy of valid license/registration/ empanelment from the relevant Government authority as applicable for one or more Applications/solution/ services mentioned in 5(3).

(continued)

(continued)

S.N.	Type of vertical	Minimum Qualifying Criteria	Documents Required
6	Semiconductor components designer/manufacturer	1. The applicant Company should be registered in India	1. Copies of Registration, PAN and GST Certificate
		2. Semiconductor components design/manufacturing and ICT measuring Instruments manufacturing/supply should be one of the objectives listed in the MoA (or a legally equivalent document) of the applicant company.	2. As a proof of turnover balance sheet or relevant pages from annual report indicating the turnover of the applicant company duly certified by a director or company secretary.
		3. The applicant company should be in the business of Semiconductor components design/manufacturing, ICT measuring Instruments manufacturing/supply	3. Certified copy of MoA of the applicant company highlighting provision of one or more activity as mentioned in 6(3) as an objective.
			4. Self-declaration that the semiconductor components manufacturing is done by the applicant company in a plant in India (Details of Plant location and its registration to be provided).
			5. If manufacturing is outsourced:
			i. Copy of certificate of registration of the company owning the plant and manufacturing the product of the applicant company.
			ii. Copy of Registration of the plant.
			iii. Invoice copy raised from the company owning plant to the applicant company (Financial figures can be masked).
			6. In case applicant company is involved only in design:
			i. A self certified certificate that the company is in the business of designing of semiconductor components (Name and range of products to be mentioned)

(continued)

(continued)

S.N.	Type of vertical	Minimum Qualifying Criteria	Documents Required
7	Terminal Equipment Manufacturers: Manufacturers of Mobile Device / CPE/ End User	1. The applicant Company should be registered in India 2. The Manufacturing of Terminal Equipment Manufacturers: Manufacturers of Mobile Device / CPE/ End User should be one of the objectives listed in the MoA (or a legally equivalent document) of the applicant company 3. The applicant should be engaged in manufacturing of Terminal Equipment Manufacturers: Manufacturers of Mobile Device / CPE/ End User through its own facility in India or through contract manufacturing in India	1. Copies of Registration, PAN and GST Certificate 2. As a proof of turnover balance sheet or relevant pages from annual report indicating the turnover of the applicant company duly certified by a director or company secretary. 3. Name of the product being manufactured and copy of MoA of the applicant company highlighting manufacturing as an objective as per 7(3). 4. Self-declaration that the telecom equipment is manufactured by the applicant company in a plant in India (Details of Plant location and its registration to be provided). 5. If manufacturing is outsourced: i. Copy of certificate of registration of the company owning the plant and manufacturing the product of the applicant company. ii. Copy of Registration of the plant. iii. Invoice copy raised from the company owning plant to the applicant company (Financial figures can be masked).
8	R&D organizations	1. The applicant Company/entity should be registered in India 2. R&D should be the primary activity of the organisation as stated in the MoA and it should be recognised/ accredited as a R&D institution by the Government of India.	1. Copies of Registration, PAN and GST Certificate 2. As a proof of turnover Balance Sheet or relevant pages from annual report indicating the turnover of the applicant company duly certified by a director or company secretary. 3. If the R&D organization is registered as not for profit organisation, a certificate to that effect is required to be provided. 4. Government Authority/ DSIR Certificate recognizing the organization as R&D organisation 5. Copy of MoA/AoA highlighting that the main line of activity of the organisation is Research and Development
9	Academic Institutions	Indian academic institutions having courses in telecommunication engineering / IT/ Computer engineering/ technology/ management etc. recognized/ accredited by appropriate authority in India.	1. Copies of Registration, PAN and GST Certificate 2. Self-declaration accompanied by a copy of MoA highlighting that the applicant is an Academic Institution 3. Accreditation certificate from requisite Govt. Authority in India 4. List of courses which include courses mentioned in column

(continued)

(continued)

S.N.	Type of vertical	Minimum Qualifying Criteria	Documents Required
10	Government Department/ Statutory or Autonomous bodies/organisations set up by the Government or Statutory or autonomous bodies	Following organisations under Central/State Government: 1. Central/State Government Ministries/ Departments/Institutions 2. Organisations owned or controlled by Central/ State Government 3. Organisations set up by statutory/autonomous bodies	1. The application should be forwarded along with a signed communication on official letterhead of the Govt departments/bodies/entities with organisation seal 2. In case the organisation is a registered entity: Certified copies of Registration, PAN and GST Certificate
11	Any other entity in ICT enabled product manufacturing/ service/ solution provider domain (not covered elsewhere)	The applicant Company/entity should be registered in India 1. The applicant should be engaged in the business of products manufacturing/service/solution provider domain listed in the column 'Type of vertical' through its own facility in India with applicable accreditation/registration/license or any other applicable approval in India.	1. Copies of Registration, PAN and GST Certificate 2. As a proof of turnover balance sheet or relevant pages from annual report indicating the turnover of the applicant company duly certified by a director or company secretary. 3. Certified copy of Valid license/registration/ empanelment from the relevant Government authority as applicable for one or more out of manufacturing/service/solution mentioned in 11(1) or Copy of MoA highlighting main line of business 4. In case of manufacturing unit: i. Registration certificate of the plant in India ii. Invoice copy raised from the plant (Financial figures can be masked).
12	Associate Membership	1. Association of Indian stakeholders / Entity	1. Copies of Registration, PAN and GST Certificate 2. MOA/AOA or any other document highlighting the main line of business / activity. 3. Copy of latest Annual Report
		2. Association of Foreign stakeholders / Entity	1. Certificate of Incorporation 2. MOA/AOA or any other document highlighting the main line of business / activity. 3. Copy of latest Annual Report

Note:

1. All certificates/documents should be self-attested unless specific authorisation required as mentioned in the table above.
2. TSDSI may seek clarification in support of eligibility requirements.

Annexure II: IPR Licensing Declaration Form for TSDSI

TSDSI

APPENDIX

IPR LICENSING DECLARATION FORMS

IPR HOLDER/ORGANISATION ("Declarant")

Legal Name:

CONTACT DETAILS FOR LICENSING

INFORMATION Name and Title:

Department:

Address:

Telephone: Fax:

Email: URL:

GENERAL IPR LICENSING

DECLARATION

In accordance with Clause 5.1 of the TSDSI IPR POLICY the Declarant and/or its AFFILIATES hereby informs TSDSI that *(check one box only):*
    with reference to TSDSI STANDARD(s) or TECHNICAL SPECIFICATION(s) no. _____, or with reference to TSDSI Project(s): _____, or with reference to all TSDSI STANDARDS and TECHNICAL

SPECIFICATIONS and with reference to *(check one box only):*

© The Editor(s) (if applicable) and The Author(s) 2022
V. H. Bharadwaj et al., *Locating Legal Certainty in Patent Licensing*,
https://doi.org/10.1007/978-981-15-0181-4

IPR(s) contained within technical contributions made by the Declarant and/or its AFFILIATES, or any IPRs the Declarant hereby irrevocably declares that 1) it and/or its AFFILIATES are prepared to grant irrevocable licenses under its/their IPR(s) on terms and conditions which are in accordance with the provisions of Clause 5.1 of TSDSI's IPR POLICY, in respect of the STANDARD(S), TECHNICAL SPECIFI-CATION(S), or the TSDSI project(s), as identified above, to the extent that the IPR(s) are or become, and remain ESSENTIAL to practice that/those STANDARD(S) or TECHNICAL SPECIFICATION(S) or, as applicable, any STANDARD or TECH-NICAL SPECIFICATION resulting from proposals or Work Items within the current scope of the above identified TSDSI project(s), for the field of use of practice of such STANDARD or TECHNICAL SPECIFICATION; and 2) it will comply with Clause 5.3 of TSDSI's IPR Policy with respect to such ESSENTIAL IPR(s).

This irrevocable undertaking is made subject to the condition that those who seek licences agree to reciprocate **(check box if applicable).**

The construction, validity and performance of this General IPR licensing declaration shall be governed by the laws of India.

Terms in ALL CAPS on this form have the meaning provided in Clause 2 of the TSDSI IPR POLICY.

SIGNATURE

Note: By signing this General IPR Licensing Declaration form, you represent that you have the authority to bind the Declarant and/or its AFFILIATES to the representations and commitments provided in this form.

Name of authorized person:

Title of authorized person:

Place, Date:

Signature:

Please return this form duly signed to: TSDSI Director-General

Annexure III: IPR Information Statement and Licensing Declaration for TSDSI

TSDSI

IPR INFORMATION STATEMENT AND LICENSING DECLARATION

IPR HOLDER / ORGANISATION ("Declarant")

Legal Name:

CONTACT DETAILS FOR LICENSING INFORMATION

Name and Title:

Department:

Address:

Telephone: Fax:

Email: URL:

IPR INFORMATION STATEMENT

> In accordance with Clause 5.1 of the TSDSI IPR POLICY the Declarant and/or its AFFILIATES hereby informs TSDSI that it is the Declarant's and/or its AFFILIATES' present belief that the IPR(s) disclosed in the attached *IPR Information Statement Annex* may be or may become ESSENTIAL in relation to at least the TSDSI Work Item(s), STANDARD(S) and/or TECHNICAL SPECIFICATIONS identified in the attached *IPR Information Statement Annex.*

The Declarant and/or its AFFILIATES (*check one box only*):

are the proprietor(s) of the IPR(s) disclosed in the attached *IPR Information Statement Annex.* are not the proprietor(s) of the IPR(s) disclosed in the attached *IPR Information Statement Annex.*

© The Editor(s) (if applicable) and The Author(s) 2022
V. H. Bharadwaj et al., *Locating Legal Certainty in Patent Licensing*,
https://doi.org/10.1007/978-981-15-0181-4

IPR LICENSING DECLARATION [if Declarant is IPR owner]

In accordance with Clause 5.1 of the TSDSI IPR POLICY the Declarant and/or its AFFILIATES hereby irrevocably declares the following (**check one box only, and subordinate box, where applicable**):

To the extent that the IPR(s) disclosed in the attached IPR Information Statement Annex are or become, and remain ESSENTIAL in respect of the TSDSI Work Item, STANDARD and/or TECHNICAL SPECIFICATION identified in the attached IPR Information Statement Annex, the Declarant and/or its AFFILIATES are 1) prepared to grant irrevocable licences under this/these IPR(s) on terms and conditions which are in accordance with Clause 5.1 of the TSDSI IPR POLICY; and 2) will comply with Clause 5.3 of the TSDSI IPR POLICY.

This irrevocable undertaking is made subject to the condition that those who seek licences agree to reciprocate (*check box if applicable*).

The Declarant and/or its AFFILIATES are not prepared to make the above IPR Licensing Declaration (reasons may be explained in writing in the attached *IPR Licensing Declaration Annex*).

The construction, validity and performance of this IPR information statement and licensing declaration shall be governed by the laws of India.

Terms in ALL CAPS on this form have the meaning provided in Clause 2 of the TSDSI IPR POLICY.

SIGNATURE

Note: By signing this IPR Information Statement and Licensing Declaration form, you represent that you have the authority to bind the Declarant and/or its AFFILIATES to the representations and commitments provided in this form.

Name of authorized person:

Title of authorized person:

Place, Date:

Signature:

Please return this form duly signed to TSDSI

Annexure IV: IPR Information Statement for TSDSI

TSDSI

IPR INFORMATION STATEMENT

Standard, technical specification or TSDSI project item				Proprietor Title	Application No.	Publication No.	Patent/Application	Patent No. If granted	Country of registration	Additional Information Other members of this Patent Family, if any*		
Project or Standard Name	Work Item or Standard No.	Specification part of the standard (e.g. Section)	Version (V.X.X .X)							Application No..	Publication No	Country of registration

* Additional Information on IPR applications in India and other countries related to other members of a Patent Family is provided voluntarily.

Members may use the space below (or provide additional sheet duly signed) to provide Uniform Resource Locators (URL or link), pointing to the disclosures made by their AFFILIATES to any other standard body.

Please return this form together with the "IPR Information Statement and Licensing Declaration form" to TSDSI Director-General

© The Editor(s) (if applicable) and The Author(s) 2022
V. H. Bharadwaj et al., *Locating Legal Certainty in Patent Licensing*,
https://doi.org/10.1007/978-981-15-0181-4

Annexure V: IPR Licensing Declaration for TSDSI

TSDSI

IPR LICENSING DECLARATION

Optional written explanation of reasons for not making the IPR Licensing Declaration

The Declarant and/or its AFFILIATES are unwilling to grant irrevocable licences under the IPR(s) disclosed in the attached IPR Information Statement Annex on terms and conditions which are in accordance with Clause 4.1 of the TSDSI IPR POLICY.0

The Declarant and/or its AFFILIATES are unable to grant irrevocable licences under the IPR(s) disclosed in the attached IPR Information Statement Annex on terms and conditions which are in accordance with Clause 4.1 of the TSDSI IPR POLICY, because

the Declarant and/or its AFFILIATES are not the proprietor of the IPR(s) disclosed in the attached *IPR Information Statement Annex,*

the Declarant and/or its AFFILIATES do not have the ability to licence the IPR(s) disclosed in the attached *IPR Information Statement Annex* on terms and conditions which are in accordance with Clause 4.1 of the TSDSI IPR POLICY. In this case, please provide Contact information of those who may have this ability:

Legal Name:

Name and Title:

Department:

Address:

Telephone: Fax:

V. H. Bharadwaj et al., *Locating Legal Certainty in Patent Licensing*,
https://doi.org/10.1007/978-981-15-0181-4

Email:

Other reasons (please specify):

Please return this form together with the "IPR Information Statement and Licensing Declaration Form" to TSDSI Director-General,

Annexure VI: Application for ETSI Membership

Application for ETSI Membership[1]

Corporate email address to receive acknowledgement of Membership application.

Email address:

Confirmation:

Legally established, registered **name and address** of the applicant Administration / Organization

Please enter short and long name (even if it is the same)

Short name

Long name :

Phone: ww w:

Addr ess:

---

[1] The Form is only available online at <https://portal.etsi.org/membership_app/applicationform. aspx>

Addr
ess(2
):

Addr
ess(3
):

Addr
ess(4
):

Posta ———— City ———— Cou
l cod   ntry
e: :   :

Membership status (Full, Associate or Observer Membership)

(•)   Legally established in a country within the CEPT* geographical area (Full Membership)

○   Legally established in a country outside the CEPT* geographical area (Associate Membership)

○   Eligible for Full or Associate Membership but choosing no participation in technical work (Observer
Membership)

* CEPT - European Conference of Postal and Telecommunications Administrations

Active in the following area

Represented by (person who is legally responsible for the company)

                First ———— Last   Pos
Title: na   na   itio
                me: me: n:

cognizant of the ETSI Directives available at http://portal.etsi.org/Directives/home.asp **hereby applies
for   ETSI   Membership   in   the   category   of**

Category: Type field:

and also applies to participate in 3GPP™ (subject to minimum contribution) ○ Yes (•) No

Information   related   to   contacts

You can overwrite the pre-filled fields, if the official contact's details are different.

Name and address of **Official Contact** - the main contact between an ETSI Member Organization and the ETSI Secretariat, to whom all correspondence is sent and who is responsible for the maintenance of that organization's membership data.

Title: | First nam e: | Last nam e: |

Phon e: | E- mail :

Addr ess:

Addr ess (2):

Addr ess (3):

Addr ess (4):

Posta l cod e: | City: | Cou ntry:

⌐ Financial Contact is not the same as Official Contact

⌐ Billing address is not the same as Organization's/Administration's address

Invoices to be sent to the

(•) Official contact   ○ Financial contact   ○ Billing address   ○ Organization's address   ○ Other addres

European Union VAT N°

Information related to the Membership fee

Administrations

If another Administration in your country is already an ETSI Member and pays Membership fees according to the

Gross Domestic Product (GDP) of your country, please tick this box ⌐

If your Administration is responsible for the regulation of electronics communications and related areas in that country, please indicate your country's GDP in billion €.

Billion   €

If none of the above cases apply, but you are a governmental body, please tick this box ⌐

Members' fees are calculated by class based on the declared ECRT (Electronics Communications Related Turnover).

Each class corresponds to a number of units/voting weights. This number determines the contribution payable. SMEs, User/Trade associations, Universities and Public Research Bodies come under class 1.

Organization
Please   indicate   your   organization's   annual **ECRT** in   million   €.
In the case where the member's ECRT is not able to be determined from publicly available information, the member will agree with the Director-General on the appropriate Class of Contribution which should apply.

Million € [   ]   or   [▼]

Additional   **Membership**
If you are applying for an **Additional Membership** to an existing Group Membership for which the membership fees have already been determined. Please provide the **NAME OF THE ORGANIZATION** holding the relevant

Group Membership : [   ]

The applicant Administration / Organization hereby agrees and commits itself to comply with the provisions of the ETSI Directives and all decisions taken by the ETSI General Assembly, to contribute to the work, to make use of the standards produced to the extent practicable and to support those standards for use as the basis for world standards   and   recommendations.
By signing this application form, you represent that you have the legal authority to bind the applicant Administration/Organization to the representations and commitments provided in this application form.
Membership of ETSI will be tacitly renewed unless it is withdrawn before 30th September of the current year by the Member Organization (see Rules of Procedure, Article 1, clause 1.4.1 for full details).

Read and approved on behalf of the Administration / Organization:

⌐ I agree and accept that all personal data (related to my organisation legal representative and/or official contact and/or financial contact status) contained in the present form are collected and stored in compliance with the ETSI privacy policy to have access to ETSI services as long as I hold an ETSI membership.

If you have any question about your personal data or wish to exercise your rights of access, rectification and/or erasure, please send an e-mail to privacy@etsi.org.

Name and Title of authorized signatory: [   ]

Verification code
Please copy the code from the image into the text field:

K2J2W

Note: when you have submitted the form you will get a printable version.

In order to accelerate the process please email the printed and signed (scanned) version to **Membership@etsi.org**
Until the application has been processed and validated by the Membership team you can still make modifications by connecting to the online application form via an URL sent to you by e-mail.

To complete the membership application please print the form, sign it and post it to:
ETSI Membership, 650 route des Lucioles, 06921 Sophia Antipolis Cedex, FRANCE
For any question, you may contact **membership@etsi.org** or call at **+33 4 9294 4269**
I confirm the accuracy of this information and submit the form

Help | French Translation

Annexure VII: IPR Licensing Declaration Form for ETSI

RULES OF PROCEDURE, 3 September 2020

ANNEX 6 - Appendix A: **IPR Licensing Declaration forms**

IPR HOLDER / ORGANISATION ("Declarant")

Legal Name:

CONTACT DETAILS FOR LICENSING INFORMATION:

Name and Title:

Department:

Address:

Telephone: Fax:

Email: URL:

GENERAL IPR LICENSING DECLARATION

In accordance with Clause 6.1 of the ETSI IPR Policy the Declarant and/or its AFFILIATES hereby informs ETSI that (**check one box only**):

☐ with reference to ETSI STANDARD(S) or TECHNICAL SPECIFICATION(S) No.: _____,
or
☐ with reference to ETSI Project(s): _____, or
☐ with reference to all ETSI STANDARDS AND TECHNICAL SPECIFICA-TIONS

and with reference to (check one box only):

☐ IPR(s) contained within technical contributions made by the Declarant and/or its AFFILIATES, or any IPRs

© The Editor(s) (if applicable) and The Author(s) 2022
V. H. Bharadwaj et al., *Locating Legal Certainty in Patent Licensing*,
https://doi.org/10.1007/978-981-15-0181-4

☐ the Declarant hereby irrevocably declares that (1) it and its AFFILIATES are prepared to grant irrevocable licenses under its/their IPR(s) on terms and conditions which are in accordance with Clause 6.1 of the ETSI IPR Policy, in respect of the STANDARD(S), TECHNICAL SPECIFICATION(S), or the ETSI Project(s), as identified above, to the extent that the IPR(s) are or become, and remain ESSENTIAL to practice that/those STANDARD(S) or TECHNICAL SPECIFI-CATION(S) or, as applicable, any STANDARD or TECHNICAL SPECIFICA-TION resulting from proposals or Work Items within the current scope of the above identified ETSI Project(s), for the field of use of practice of such STAN-DARD or TECHNICAL SPECIFICATION; and (2) it will comply with Clause 6.1bis of the ETSI IPR Policy with respect to such ESSENTIAL IPR(s).

This irrevocable undertaking is made subject to the condition that those who seek licences agree to reciprocate (**check box if applicable**).

☐ The construction, validity and performance of this General IPR licensing declaration shall be governed by the laws of France.

Terms in ALL CAPS on this form have the meaning provided in Clause 15 of the ETSI IPR Policy.

SIGNATURE

By signing this General IPR Licensing Declaration form, you represent that you have the authority to bind the Declarant and/or its AFFILIATES to the representations and commitments provided in this form.

Name of authorized person:

Title of authorized person:

Place, Date:

Signature:

Please return this form duly signed to: Director-General ETSI - 650, route des Lucioles - F-06921 Sophia Antipolis Cedex – France / Fax. +33 (0) 4 93 65 47 16

Annexure VIII: Statement and Licensing Declaration Form for ETSI

RULES OF PROCEDURE, 3 September 2020

STATEMENT AND LICENSING DECLARATION

IPR HOLDER / ORGANISATION ("Declarant")

Legal Name:

CONTACT DETAILS FOR LICENSING INFORMATION:

Name and Title:

Department:

Address:

Telephone: Fax:

Email: URL:

IPR INFORMATION STATEMENT

In accordance with Clause 4.1 of the ETSI IPR Policy the Declarant and/or its AFFIL-IATES hereby informs ETSI that it is the Declarant's and/or its AFFILIATES' present belief that the IPR(s) disclosed in the attached IPR Information Statement Annex may be or may become ESSENTIAL in relation to at least the ETSI Work Item(s), STAN-DARD(S) and/or TECHNICAL SPECIFICATION(S) identified in the attached IPR Information Statement Annex.

The Declarant and/or its AFFILIATES (check one box only):

☐ are the proprietor of the IPR(s) disclosed in the attached IPR Information Statement Annex.

☐ are not the proprietor of the IPR(s) disclosed in the attached IPR Information Statement Annex.

V. H. Bharadwaj et al., *Locating Legal Certainty in Patent Licensing*,
https://doi.org/10.1007/978-981-15-0181-4

IPR LICENSING DECLARATION

In accordance with Clause 6.1 of the ETSI IPR Policy the Declarant and/or its AFFILIATES hereby irrevocably declares the following (check one box only, and subordinate box, where applicable):

☐ To the extent that the IPR(s) disclosed in the attached IPR Information Statement Annex are or become, and remain ESSENTIAL in respect of the ETSI Work Item, STANDARD and/or TECHNICAL SPECIFICATION identified in the attached IPR Information Statement Annex, the Declarant and/or its AFFILIATES are (1) prepared to grant irrevocable licences under this/these IPR(s) on terms and conditions which are in accordance with Clause 6.1 of the ETSI IPR Policy; and (2) will comply with Clause 6.1bis of the ETSI IPR Policy.

   ☐ This irrevocable undertaking is made subject to the condition that those who seek licences agree to reciprocate (check box if applicable).

☐ The Declarant and/or its AFFILIATES are not prepared to make the above IPR Licensing Declaration (reasons may be explained in writing in the attached IPR Licensing Declaration Annex).

The construction, validity and performance of this IPR information statement and licensing declaration shall be governed by the laws of France.

Terms in ALL CAPS on this form have the meaning provided in Clause 15 of the ETSI IPR Policy.

SIGNATURE

By signing this IPR Information Statement and Licensing Declaration form, you represent that you have the authority to bind the Declarant and/or its AFFILIATES to the representations and commitments provided in this form.

Name of authorized person:

Title of authorized person:

Place, Date:

Signature:

Please return this form duly signed to: Director-General ETSI - 650, route des Lucioles - F-06921 Sophia Antipolis Cedex – France / Fax. +33 (0) 4 93 65 47 16

Annexure IX: ETSI - IPR Information Statement Annex

ETSI - IPR Information Statement Annex

STANDARD, TECHNICAL SPECIFICATION or ETSI Work Item				Propr ietor	Applic ation No.	Public ation No.	Patent/Ap plication Title	Country of registrat ion	FURTHER INFORMATION Other members of this PATENT FAMILY, if any *		
Proj ect or Stan dard nam e	Wor k Item or Stan dard No.	Illustr ative Specif ic part of the stand ard (e.g. Sectio n)	Versi on (V.X. X.X)						Applic ation No.	Public ation No.	Count ry of registr ation
e.g. UMT S	ETSI TS 125 215	6.1.1. 2	V.3.5. 0	Abcd		EP 11319 72	Scheduling of slotted-mode related measureme nts	EPC CONTRA CTING STATES		AU 12740/ 00	Austra lia
										CN 99813 100.8	China P.R.
										FI 10827 0	Finlan d
										JP 11-31816 1	Japan
										US 65322 26	USA

© The Editor(s) (if applicable) and The Author(s) 2022
V. H. Bharadwaj et al., *Locating Legal Certainty in Patent Licensing*,
https://doi.org/10.1007/978-981-15-0181-4

* Information on other members of a PATENT FAMILY is provided voluntarily (Clause 4.3 of the ETSI IPR Policy).

Please return this form together with the "IPR Information Statement and Licensing Declaration form" to:

ETSI Director-General - ETSI - 650, route des Lucioles - F-06921 Sophia Antipolis Cedex – France / Fax. +33 (0) 4 93 65 47 16

Annexure X: Optional Written Explanation of Reasons for Not Making the IPR Licensing Declaration

ETSI IPR Licensing Declaration Annex ETSI IPR POLICY

Optional written explanation of reasons for not making the IPR Licensing Declaration

☐ The Declarant and/or its AFFILIATES are unwilling to grant irrevocable licences under the IPR(s) disclosed in the attached IPR Information Statement Annex on terms and conditions which are in accordance with Clause 6.1 of the ETSI IPR Policy.

☐ The Declarant and/or its AFFILIATES are unable to grant irrevocable licences under the IPR(s) disclosed in the attached IPR Information Statement Annex on terms and conditions which are in accordance with Clause 6.1 of the ETSI IPR Policy, because

    ☐ the Declarant and/or its AFFILIATES are not the proprietor of the IPR(s) disclosed in the attached IPR Information Statement Annex,

    ☐ the Declarant and/or its AFFILIATES do not have the ability to licence the IPR(s) disclosed in the attached IPR Information Statement Annex on terms and conditions which are in accordance with Clause 6.1 of the ETSI IPR Policy. In this case, please provide Contact information of those who may have this ability:

        Legal Name:
        Name and Title:
        Department:
        Address:
        Telephone:
        Fax:
        Email:

☐ Other reasons (please specify):

© The Editor(s) (if applicable) and The Author(s) 2022
V. H. Bharadwaj et al., *Locating Legal Certainty in Patent Licensing*,
https://doi.org/10.1007/978-981-15-0181-4

Please return this form together with the "IPR Information Statement and Licensing Declaration form" to: Director-General ETSI - 650, route des Lucioles - F-06921 Sophia Antipolis Cedex – France / Fax. +33 (0) 4 93 65 47 16

Annexure XI: Letter of Assurance for Essential Patent Claims for IEEE

LETTER OF ASSURANCE FOR ESSENTIAL PATENT CLAIMS

Please return via mail,	PatCom Administrator, IEEE-SA Standards Board Patent
Committee e-mail (as a PDF), or fax:	Institute of Electrical and Electronics Engineers, Inc.
	445 Hoes Lane
	Piscataway, NJ 08854 USA
	FAX (+1 732-875-0524) e-mail: patcom@ieee.org

> *No license is implied by submission of this Letter of Assurance*

A. SUBMITTER:

Legal Name:_____("Submitter")

B. SUBMITTER'S CONTACT INFORMATION:

Contact
Name/Title: _____
Department: _____
Address: _____
_____ Fax: _____ E-mail: _____
Telephone
: URL:

© The Editor(s) (if applicable) and The Author(s) 2022
V. H. Bharadwaj et al., *Locating Legal Certainty in Patent Licensing*,
https://doi.org/10.1007/978-981-15-0181-4

Note: The IEEE does not endorse the content, or confirm the accuracy or consistency of any contact information or web site listed above.

C. IEEE STANDARD OR PROJECT (e.g., AMENDMENT, CORRIGENDUM, OR REVISION):

In accordance with Clause 6 of the *IEEE-SA Standards Board Bylaws* and Clause 6.3.5 of the *IEEE-SA Standards Board Operations Manual*, this licensing position is limited to the following:

Standard/Project
Number: Title:

D. SUBMITTER'S POSITION REGARDING LICENSING OF ESSENTIAL PATENT CLAIMS:

In accordance with Clause 6 of the *IEEE-SA Standards Board Bylaws*, the Submitter hereby declares the following

(Check box 1 or box 2 below):

Note: Nothing in this Letter of Assurance shall be interpreted as giving rise to a duty to conduct a patent search. The IEEE takes no position with respect to the validity or essentiality of Patent Claims, determining whether an implementation is a Compliant Implementation or the reasonableness of rates, terms, and conditions provided in connection with submission of a Letter of Assurance, if any, or in any license agreements offered by the Submitter. To the extent there are inconsistencies between the Letter of Assurance Form and any sample licenses, material licensing terms, or not to exceed rates provided in connection with 1.a or 1.b below, the terms of Clause 6 of the IEEE-SA Standards Board Bylaws and this Letter of Assurance Form shall control.

☐ 1. The Submitter may own, control, or have the ability to license Patent Claims that might be or become Essential Patent Claims. With respect to such Essential Patent Claims, the Submitter's licensing position is as follows *(must check a, b, c, or d and any applicable subordinate boxes):*

    ☐ a. The Submitter will make available a license for Essential Patent Claims without compensation to an unrestricted number of Applicants on a worldwide basis with other reasonable terms and conditions that are demonstrably free of unfair discrimination to make, have made, use, sell, offer to sell, or import any Compliant Implementation that practices the Essential Patent Claims for use in conforming with the IEEE Standard identified in part C.

      ☐   (Optional) A sample of such a license (or material licensing terms) that is substantially similar to what the Submitter would offer is attached.

      ☐   (Optional) Such a license will include a Reciprocal Licensing requirement.

☐ b. The Submitter will make available a license for Essential Patent Claims under Reasonable Rates to an unrestricted number of Applicants on a worldwide basis with other reasonable terms and conditions that are demonstrably free of unfair discrimination to make, have made, use, sell, offer to sell, or import any Compliant Implementation that practices the Essential Patent Claims for use in conforming with the IEEE Standard identified in part C.

                                              _____

      ☐   (Optional) These reasonable rates will not exceed of unit price, flat fee, per unit).

         (e.g., percent)

      ☐   (Optional) A sample of such a license (or material licensing terms) that is substantially similar to what the Submitter would offer is attached.

      ☐   (Optional) Such a license will include a Reciprocal Licensing requirement.

☐ c. The Submitter without conditions will not enforce any present or future Essential Patent Claims against any person or entity making, having made, using, selling, offering to sell, or importing any Compliant Implementation that practices the Essential Patent Claims for use in conforming with the IEEE Standard identified in part C.

☐ d. The Submitter is unwilling or unable to grant licenses according to the provisions of either a or b above or to agree that it will not enforce its Essential Patent Claims as described in c above. This statement applies to the Patent Claims identified in E.1 below.

☐ 2. After a Reasonable and Good Faith Inquiry, the Submitter is not aware of any Patent Claims that the Submitter may own, control, or have the ability to license that might be or become Essential Patent Claims.

E. SCOPE OF ASSURANCE:

Note: The Submitter must complete this section if box 1 in part D above is checked.

The Submitter may, but is not required to, identify one or more of its Patent Claims that it believes might be or become Essential Patent Claims. (***Submitter must check box 1 or box 2 below***)

☐ 3. When checked, this Letter of Assurance only applies to the Patent Claims identified below that are or become Essential Patent Claims. (If no Patent Claim is identified below, then this Letter of Assurance applies to all Essential Patent Claims supported by the disclosure in the patent or patent applications listed below.)

Patent/Application/Docket
Number: Description/Title
(optional):

Claim (optional):

Patent/Application/Docket
Number: Description/Title
(optional):

Claim (optional):

Patent/Application/Docket Number:
Description/Title (optional):

Claim (optional):

For additional patents, use additional pages as necessary.

☐ 4. When checked, this Letter of Assurance is a Blanket Letter of Assurance. As such, all Essential Patent Claims that the Submitter may currently or in the future have the ability to license shall be available under the terms as indicated in part D.1; however, a Blanket Assurance shall not supersede any pre- existing or simultaneously submitted specific assurance identifying potential Essential Patent Claims.

F. APPLICATION TO AFFILIATES:

With respect to any Essential Patent Claims that an Affiliate has the ability to license, the Submitter agrees that (i) the licensing positions described in parts C and D apply to any Essential Patent Claims within the scope of the assurance described in part E; and (ii) the terms of this assurance are binding on each such Affiliate; provided, however, that such representations and commitments shall not apply to Affiliates identified below:

identified below:

Organization's Name		Organization's Name
Address		Address
Contact person		Contact person

Affiliates may not be excluded if the Reciprocal Licensing box is checked in part D.1.a or D.1.b. For additional Affiliates, use additional pages as necessary.

G. SIGNATURE:

By signing this Letter of Assurance, you represent that you have the authority to bind the Submitter and all Affiliates (other than those Affiliates permissibly excluded above) to the representations and commitments provided in this LOA and acknowledge that users and implementers of the IEEE Standard identified in part C are relying or will rely upon and may seek enforcement of the terms of this LOA. The Submitter and all Affiliates (other than those Affiliates permissibly excluded above) agree not to sell or otherwise transfer any rights in any Essential Patent Claims that they hold, control, or have the ability to license with the intent of circumventing or negating any of the representations and commitments made in this LOA.

The Submitter agrees (a) to provide notice of an Accepted Letter of Assurance either through a Statement of Encumbrance or by binding its assignee or transferee to the terms of such Letter of Assurance; and (b) to require its assignee or transferee to (i) agree to similarly provide such notice and (ii) to bind its assignees or transferees to agree to provide such notice as described in (a) and (b).

If D.1.a or D.1.b is checked, the Submitter shall not condition a license on the Applicant's agreeing (a) to grant a license to any of the Applicant's Patent Claims that are not Essential Patent Claims for the IEEE Standard identified in part C, or (b) to take a license for any of the Submitter's Patent Claims that are not Essential Patent Claims for the IEEE Standard identified in part C.

If, as described in Clause 6 of the *IEEE-SA Standards Board Bylaws*, the Submitter becomes aware of additional Patent Claims not already covered by an Accepted Letter of Assurance that are owned, controlled, or licensable by the Submitter and that may be or become Essential Patent Claims with respect to the IEEE Standard identified in part C, the Submitter agrees to submit a Letter of Assurance stating its position regarding enforcement or licensing of such Patent Claims.

Print name of authorized person:

Title of authorized person:

Signature of authorized person:

Address:

Phone: E-mail:

Note that this assurance applies, at a minimum, from the date of the standard's approval to the date of the standard's transfer to inactive status and is irrevocable upon acceptance by the IEEE-SA.

The IEEE-SA Patent Policy and the procedures used to execute that policy are documented in the IEEE-SA Standards Board Bylaws and the IEEE-SA Standards Board Operations Manual, available at https://standards.ieee.org/about/policies/index.html. The terms and definitions set forth in the IEEE-SA Patent Policy, IEEE-SA Standards Board Bylaws, and IEEE-SA Standards Board Operations Manual in effect as of the date of this Letter of Assurance are incorporated herein.

DEFINITIONS

The following terms, when capitalized, have the following meanings:

"Accepted Letter of Assurance" and *"Accepted LOA"* shall mean a Letter of Assurance that the IEEE-SA has determined is complete in all material respects and has been posted to the IEEE-SA web site.

"Affiliate" shall mean an entity that directly or indirectly, through one or more intermediaries, controls the Submitter or Applicant, is controlled by the Submitter or Applicant, or is under common control with the Submitter or Applicant. For the purposes of this definition, the term "control" and its derivatives, with respect to for-profit entities, means the legal, beneficial or equitable ownership, directly or indirectly, of more than fifty percent (50%) of the capital stock (or other ownership interest, if not a corporation) of an entity ordinarily having voting rights. "Control" and its derivatives, with respect to nonprofit entities, means the power to elect or appoint more than fifty percent (50%) of the Board of Directors of an entity.

"Applicant" shall mean any prospective licensee for Essential Patent Claims. *"Applicant"* shall include all of its Affiliates.

"Blanket Letter of Assurance" shall mean a Letter of Assurance that applies to all Essential Patent Claims for which a Submitter may currently or in the future (except

as otherwise provided for in these Bylaws and in the *IEEE-SA Standards Board Operations Manual)* have the ability to license.

"*Compliant Implementation*" shall mean any product (e.g., component, sub-assembly, or end-product) or service that conforms to any mandatory or optional portion of a normative clause of an IEEE Standard.

"*Enabling Technology*" shall mean any technology that may be necessary to make or use any product or portion thereof that complies with the IEEE Standard but is neither explicitly required by nor expressly set forth in the IEEE Standard (e.g., semiconductor manufacturing technology, compiler technology, object-oriented technology, basic operating system technology, and the like).

"*Essential Patent Claim*" shall mean any Patent Claim the practice of which was necessary to implement either a mandatory or optional portion of a normative clause of the IEEE Standard when, at the time of the IEEE Standard's approval, there was no commercially and technically feasible non-infringing alternative implementation method for such mandatory or optional portion of the normative clause. An Essential Patent Claim does not include any Patent Claim that was essential only for Enabling Technology or any claim other than that set forth above even if contained in the same patent as the Essential Patent Claim.

"*Letter of Assurance*" and "*LOA*" shall mean a document, including any attachments, stating the Submitter's position regarding ownership, enforcement, or licensing of Essential Patent Claims for a specifically referenced IEEE Standard, submitted in a form acceptable to the IEEE-SA.

"*Patent Claim(s)*" shall mean one or more claims in issued patent(s) or pending patent application(s).

"*Prohibitive Order*" shall mean an interim or permanent injunction, exclusion order, or similar adjudicative directive that limits or prevents making, having made, using, selling, offering to sell, or importing a Compliant Implementation.

"*Reasonable and Good Faith Inquiry*" includes, but is not limited to, a Submitter using reasonable efforts to identify and contact those individuals who are from, employed by, or otherwise represent the Submitter and who are known to the Submitter to be current or past participants in the development process of the [Proposed] IEEE Standard identified in a Letter of Assurance, including, but not limited to, participation in a Standards Association Ballot or Working Group. If the Submitter did not or does not have any participants, then a Reasonable and Good Faith Inquiry may include, but is not limited to, the Submitter using reasonable efforts to contact individuals who are from, employed by, or represent the Submitter and who the Submitter believes are most likely to have knowledge about the technology covered by the [Proposed] IEEE Standard.

"*Reasonable Rate*" shall mean appropriate compensation to the patent holder for the practice of an Essential Patent Claim excluding the value, if any, resulting from the inclusion of that Essential Patent Claim's technology in the IEEE Standard. In addition, determination of such Reasonable Rates should include, but need not be limited to, the consideration of:

- The value that the functionality of the claimed invention or inventive feature within the Essential Patent Claim contributes to the value of the relevant functionality of the smallest saleable Compliant Implementation that practices the Essential Patent Claim.
- The value that the Essential Patent Claim contributes to the smallest saleable Compliant Implementation that practices that claim, in light of the value contributed by all Essential Patent Claims for the same IEEE Standard practiced in that Compliant Implementation.
- Existing licenses covering use of the Essential Patent Claim, where such licenses were not obtained under the explicit or implicit threat of a Prohibitive Order, and where the circumstances and resulting licenses are otherwise sufficiently comparable to the circumstances of the contemplated license.

"Reciprocal Licensing" shall mean that the Submitter of an LOA has conditioned its granting of a license for its Essential Patent Claims upon the Applicant's agreement to grant a license to the Submitter with Reasonable Rates and other reasonable licensing terms and conditions to the Applicant's Essential Patent Claims, if any, for the referenced IEEE Standard, including any amendments, corrigenda, editions, and revisions. If an LOA references an amendment or corrigendum, the scope of reciprocity includes the base IEEE Standard and its amendments, corrigenda, editions, and revisions.

"Statement of Encumbrance" shall mean a specific reference to an Accepted LOA or a general statement in the transfer or assignment agreement that the Patent Claim(s) being transferred or assigned are subject to any encumbrances that may exist as of the effective date of such agreement. An Accepted LOA is an encumbrance.

"Submitter" shall mean an individual or an organization that provides a completed Letter of Assurance. A Submitter may or may not hold Essential Patent Claims. *"Submitter"* shall include all of its Affiliates unless specifically and permissibly excluded.

Should any discrepancy exist between the definitions above and the definitions in the IEEE-SA Standards Board Bylaws clause 6.1, the definitions contained in the Bylaws shall control.